Collins

Webster's

175 YEARS OF DICTIONARY PUBLISHING

easy learning

ENGLISH

CONVERSATION

BOOK 2

HarperCollins Publishers
Westerhill Road
Bishopbriggs
Glasgow
G64 2QT

First edition 2012

Reprint 10 9 8 7 6 5 4 3 2 1 0

© HarperCollins Publishers 2012

ISBN 978-0-00-745460-0

Collins ® is a registered trademark of
HarperCollins Publishers Limited

www.collinslanguage.com

A catalog record for this book is
available from the British Library

Typeset by Q2AMedia

Audio material recorded and produced
by Knowledgeworks

Printed in Great Britain by Clays Ltd,
St Ives plc

JUN 14 2013 ω

Editorial staff

Written by:
Elizabeth Walter and Kate Woodford

U.S. adaptation: Ellen Northcutt

Editor: Lisa Sutherland

For the publisher:
Lucy Cooper
Kerry Ferguson
Elaine Higgleton

contents

contents

Grammar

Collins Websters Easy Learning English Conversation: Book 2 is a completely new type of book for learners of English of all ages. It will help you to increase your confidence in holding a conversation in English in a variety of situations.

To sound natural in a foreign language, you need to know both the words and the grammar. However, it can be difficult to put these two things together and be sure that what you are saying sounds like natural English. *Easy Learning English Conversation* has been carefully designed to give you whole sentences which you can use with confidence in all your conversations.

Collins Webster's Easy Learning English Conversation is made up of 14 units, each giving the language used in a particular situation, for instance shopping, traveling, or talking about your health.

In each unit, the language is arranged by language task, for instance "saying what you want" or "making suggestions." Clear headings help you to find what you need. "Good to know" boxes give advice about important or tricky points.

You will find examples of all the phrases covered, and the words in them are explained at the bottom of each page.

At the end of each unit is a page called "Listen for," which gives more useful phrases that you may hear or need to use in each situation. This is followed by a conversation, showing the phrases you have learned in a natural situation. You can listen to these conversations on the CD that comes with this book. The CD also contains some useful phrases you can listen to and then practice saying.

After the 14 units there is a chapter which arranges the phrases by language task. So, for example, all the phrases for "complaining" come together.

Finally, there is a grammar section, giving useful advice on important grammar points, such as how to form tenses, and the differences between count and noncount nouns.

We hope *Collins Webster's Easy Learning English Conversation* will help you speak with confidence and success. For more information about Collins, please visit us at www.collinslanguage.com.

Talking to people

talking to people

Hello

You will often want to talk to people and get to know them better. The phrases in this unit will help you to speak naturally to friends, family, colleagues, and people that you meet in everyday situations.

Greetings

Use **Hello** as a general greeting. It is polite to say **Hello** to anyone in any situation.

> **Hello**, Jorge.

Use **Hi** in informal situations, for example when you are meeting friends.

> **Hi**, how are things with you?
> Oh **hi**, Adam. I didn't know you were coming.

Use **Good morning**, **Good afternoon**, or **Good evening** in slightly more formal situations, for instance if you meet a neighbor, or when you see people at work.

> **Good morning**, everyone. Today we are going to look at phrasal verbs.
> **Good afternoon**, Mr. Kowalski.

> **GOOD TO KNOW!**
> In American English, there is no greeting starting with **Good** that is for the whole day.

Use **Goodbye** when you leave someone.

> **Goodbye**, Kara. Have a safe trip.

Goodbye is often shortened to **Bye**.

> **Bye**, everyone!

Use **Goodnight** when you are going to bed, or if someone else is going to bed.

> **Goodnight**, everyone. See you in the morning.

See you is an informal way of saying goodbye to someone you know you will see again.

> **See you** later!
> OK, I need to go now. **See you**!
> **See you** on Monday!

Introducing people

If you want to introduce someone to someone else, use **This is ...** .

> **This is** my husband, Richard.
> **This is** Medina, my friend from school.
> **These are** my children, Andrew, Gordon, and Emma.

In slightly formal situations, use **I'd like you to meet ...** or **Can I introduce you to ...** ?

> **I'd like you to meet** Dr. Garcia. Dr. Garcia has been working on our project.
> **I'd like you to meet** our head of department, Elizabeth Miller.

> **Can I introduce you to** my husband, John?
> **Can I introduce you to** Omar, who's going to be giving a talk later?

GOOD TO KNOW!

When you are introduced to someone, you can just say **Hello**, or in a slightly more formal situation, say **Pleased to meet you,** or **Nice to meet you.**

Useful words
a project   a plan or piece of work that takes a lot of time and effort

Talking about yourself

When you are talking to people, you will probably want to tell them some things about you. To say what your name is, use **I'm ...** or **My name's ...** .

> Hi, **I'm** Tariq. I'm a friend of Susie's.
> **I'm** Paul. I'm your teacher for this week.

> **My name's** Johann.
> **My name's** Yuko. I'm Kazuo's sister.

To give general information about yourself, use **I'm ...** .

> **I'm** a friend of Paolo's.
> **I'm** married with two children.
> **I'm** training for the Boston Marathon.

You can also give general information about yourself using **I have ...** .

> **I have** some friends who live in Nairobi.
> **I have** relatives in Australia.
> **We have** a cabin in Maine.

To talk about your work, use **I'm** with the name of a job, or **I work** to say something more general about what you do.

> **I'm** a doctor.
> **I'm** a bus driver.

> **I work** for an oil company.
> **I work** as a translator.

Useful words

a marathon	a race in which people run a distance of 26 miles (about 42 kilometers)
a relative	a member of your family
a cabin	a small wooden house, in the woods or mountains
a translator	someone whose job is to change words into a different language

To talk about where you live, use **I live** or **I'm from**. **I'm from** is also used to talk about where you were born and lived as a child, even if you do not live there now.

> **I live** in Wales.
> **We live** near Moscow.
>
> **I'm from** Chicago originally, but I live in Phoenix now.
> **We're from** Atlanta.
> **My family's from** Guadalajara — my parents moved here in 1970.

If you are in a place for a short time, either on vacation or for work, you can say where you are living by using **I'm staying**.

> **I'm staying** at the Hotel Austin.
> **I'm staying** with friends in Budapest.
> **I'm staying** in Pusan for a week.

Asking for information

After saying **Hello** to someone, you usually ask about their health, by asking **How are you?**

> Hello, Jan. **How are you?**
> It's great to see you, Anna. **How are you?**

Useful words

originally   used for talking about something that existed or was true at
                  the beginning

To ask someone you know about their life in general, use **How are things (going)?**

> Hello, Jan. **How are things?**
> Nice to see you, Kari. **How are things going?**

When you are talking to people, and you want to ask about their life, use **Tell me ... .**

> **Tell me** about your family.
> **Tell me** a little about yourself.
> **Tell me** about your trip to Africa.

To ask someone to describe something, use **What's ... like?**

> **What's** your class **like**?
> **What's** your hometown **like**?
> **What's** your hotel **like**?

How's ... ? is used to ask someone's opinion of the quality of something, or whether they are enjoying it.

> **How's** your hotel?
> **How's** school?
> **How was** the concert?

A slightly informal way of asking someone about something they are doing is **How's ... going?**

> **How's** the new job **going**?
> **How's** your project **going**?
> **How's** it **going** at school?

Saying what you want to do

When you're talking to friends or colleagues, you will often need to talk about what you would like to do. The simplest way is to use **I'd like to ...** .

> **I'd like to** get home early tonight.
> **I'd like to** meet your family.

A slightly informal way of saying that you would like to do or have is **I wouldn't mind ...** .

> **I wouldn't mind** going to the movies.
> **I wouldn't mind** getting something to eat.

> **GOOD TO KNOW!**
> **I wouldn't mind + -ing**
> The verb that comes after **I wouldn't mind** must be in the -ing form.

Making suggestions

One easy way of making suggestions to your friends and colleagues is to use **We could ...** .

> **We could** ask Paul to join us.
> **We could** take turns introducing ourselves.

Useful words
take turns   to do something one after the other

If you are eager to do something with your friends or colleagues, use **Let's ...** .

> **Let's** all go bowling after work.
> **Let's** invite lots of people.
> **Let's** send invitations to all our colleagues.

If you want to make a suggestion and see if other people agree with you, use **Should we ...** ?

> **Should we** see what George wants to do?
> **Should we** have a working lunch?
> **Should we** ask Suri for her advice?
> **Should we** go to Jordan's party this evening?

If you have a suggestion about something you could do, use **How about ...** ? or **What about ...** ?

> **How about** going swimming?
> **How about** asking for some time off from work?
> **How about** sending him a text?

> **What about** reserving a private room?
> **What about** ordering takeout?
> **What about** buying her some flowers to say thank you?

> **GOOD TO KNOW!**
> **How about/What about + -ing**
> The verb that comes after **How about** or **What about**
> must be in the -ing form.

Useful words

bowling	a game in which you roll a heavy ball down a narrow track toward a group of wooden objects and try to knock down as many of them as possible
a working lunch	when you work at the same time you eat lunch
private	only for one particular person or group, and not for everyone
order	to ask for something to be sent to you from a company
takeout	prepared food that you buy from a shop or a restaurant and take home to eat

Another way of making a suggestion to your friends and colleagues is to use **Why don't … ?**

> **Why don't** we get together some time?
> **Why don't** we invite Martin and his brother?
> **Why don't** you meet me for lunch?
> **Why don't** you call them?

Expressing opinions

When talking to people in a social or work situation, you may want to express your opinion of something. The simplest way is to use **I think …** .

> **I think** Sonia's right.
> I don't **think** Marc's coming.

You can also use **In my opinion, …** .

> **In my opinion**, he should be fired.
> **In my opinion**, we need more staff.
> **In my opinion**, this is a great neighborhood to live in.

If you want to ask other people their opinion of something, use **What do you think of … ?** or **What do you think about … ?**

> **What do you think of** his latest movie?
> **What do you think of** Mira's new apartment?

> **What do you think about** going out for dinner tonight?
> **What do you think about** inviting Eva?

To agree with someone's opinion, use **I agree** or **You're right**. If you want to say who you agree with, use **with**.

> "This is a great restaurant." "**I agree**. We often come here."
> **I agree with** Nick.

I entirely **agree with** you!

"We'll be late if we don't hurry." "**You're right** – let's go!"
I think **you're right**.
Matt**'s right**.

If you do not agree with someone, you can use **I don't agree**. To be very polite, you might say **I'm afraid I don't agree** or **I don't really agree.**

"What a great party." "**I don't agree**. It's much too crowded and noisy."
"I thought Clara was really funny." "**I'm afraid I don't agree**. I found her jokes offensive."
"I think it's better not to invite children to weddings." "**I don't really agree**. After all, weddings are all about family."

Talking about your plans

When talking to your colleagues and friends, you may want to tell them about your plans. The simplest way is to use **I'm**, followed by a verb in the **-ing** form.

I'm seeing Phil on Thursday.
I'm having lunch with Judy.
We're getting a new computer tomorrow.

You can also use **I'm planning to ...** or, for something that you want to do, but which is not certain, **I'm hoping to ...** .

I'm planning to invite everyone I know.
I'm planning to join you later.
We're planning to open a new office in New York.

Useful words
crowded   full of people
offensive   rude or insulting

I'm **hoping to** meet her this week.
I'm **hoping to** be home by 10:00.
We're **hoping to** get a table at The Ivy.

Making arrangements

When you make arrangements with people, you may want to check if they
happy with your plan. Use **Would it work for you ... ?**

Would it work for you to have dinner at nine?
Would it work for you if I come by next week?
Would it work better **for you** if we have the meeting tomorrow?

To ask someone if they would prefer a different arrangement, use **Would you
prefer it if ... ?** or **Would it be better ... ?**

Would you prefer it if we met in town?
Would you prefer it if we ate in a restaurant?
Would you prefer it if I came to get you?

Would it be better to postpone the meeting?
Would it be better to call you in the evening?
Would it be better if we came a little earlier?

A common way to agree on the time or date of an arrangement is to use
How about ... ?

OK, **how about** next Thursday?
Lunch at Café Rouge would be great. **How about** one o'clock?
I'll meet you as soon as I finish this email – **how about** in half
an hour?

Useful words
postpone   to arrange for an event to happen at a later time

Saying what you have to do

When you want to tell your friends or colleagues that you have to do something, use **I have to ...** .

> **I have to** make a phone call.
> **We have to** be there at eight o' clock sharp.
> I really **have to** get this work finished today.
> **You** don't **have to** stay at the hotel.

To ask what someone has to do, use **Do you have to ...?**

> **Do you have to** give them an answer today?
> **Do you have to** wait for Sam?
> **Do we have to** bring something?

When you want to say that you should do something, use **I should**.

> **I should** try to reserve tickets.
> **You should** come and visit us.
> **I shouldn't** stay much longer.

Useful words
sharp   at that exact time

● Listen for

Here are some useful phrases which you may hear or want to use in conversation.

Have you ever been to Mexico City?
How long are you staying in St. Louis?
How long have you been studying English?
Your English is very good.
Am I speaking too fast?
Would you prefer it if I spoke Spanish?
Are you married?
Do you have any children?
Do you come here often?
What do you do in your free time?
Are you enjoying living here?
Have you worked here for a long time?
Could you speak a little slower, please?

Thank you for inviting me. I had a really good time.
I hope we meet again sometime.
Thank you for a lovely evening.
What a great party!
I had a great time, thanks.

 Listen to the conversation: Track 1

Brett has just started working at a hospital in San Diego. He is meeting one of his colleagues, Jim, for the first time.

A Hi, I'm Jim. I hear you've just started work here. I hope you'll enjoy it.

B Pleased to meet you. Which department are you in?

A I'm one of the physical therapists.

B How long have you been working here?

A Nearly eight years now. I'm from Los Angeles originally. How about you? Where are you from?

B I'm from Australia – Perth.

A Really? I've got relatives in Canberra – I love Australia! Where are you living at the moment?

B I'm staying at a hotel, but I'm hoping to get an apartment near the hospital. What's it like, working here?

A Pretty good. It's a friendly place. In fact, I'd like you to meet the rest of my team some time. We usually meet for dinner after work on Fridays. Why don't you join us?

B That'd be great, thanks.

A How's next Friday for you?

B Sure. I don't know anyone yet, so I'm free every night!

A OK. How about 8 o'clock, at the French restaurant on Fifth Street?

B Sounds good. See you then!

 Listen to more phrases and practice saying them: Track 2

Traveling

Have a good trip!

If you are traveling, these phrases will help you to find out how to get to places and do things such as buy tickets. They will also help you to talk about traveling in clear, natural English.

Talking about your plans

Use **I'm + -ing verb ...** or **I'm going to ...** to talk about travel plans that you are sure of.

> **I'm spending** a couple of days in Miami on the way back.
> **They're going to** take their vacation this summer, as usual.
> **I'm stopping** over in Thailand on the way there.

> **I'm going to** study in London next year.
> **I'm going to** travel first-class.
> **I'm going to** go to Kyoto this summer.

Use **Are you going to ... ?** or **Will you ... ?** to ask about someone's travel plans.

> **Are you going to** travel with Tahir?
> **Are you going to** fly there?
> **Are you going to** see Sophia while you're in Milan?

> **Will you** manage to do any sightseeing between meetings?
> **Will you** charge us extra for the bigger room?
> **Will you** call me when you get to your hotel?

Useful words

a couple	two or around two people or things
stop over	to make a stop between flights when traveling by plane
first-class	used for describing the best and most expensive seats on a train or a plane
sightseeing	visiting the interesting places that tourists go to
charge	to ask someone to pay money for something

To talk about your travel plans, you can also use **I'm planning to ...** or, if you are slightly less sure, **I'm hoping to ...** .

> **I'm planning to** spend a few days in Berlin.
> **We're planning to** drive along the coast.
> **Jack and Kim are planning to** go to Hong Kong this year.

> **I'm hoping to** stay in small hotels most of the time.
> **She's hoping to** take a tour of the nearby islands.
> **We're hoping to** fit in some skiing while we're in the Rockies.

To talk about a travel plan that is only possible, use **I might ...** .

> **I might** book a room for that night.
> **I might** spend an extra week in Calgary.
> **I might** stay on if I like it there.

To talk about something that should happen in the future, use **I'm supposed to ...** .

> **I'm supposed to** be at the station by 8:00.
> **I'm supposed to** meet Brett in Paris.
> What time **are we supposed to** get there?
> **He's supposed to** drive me to the airport.

Useful words

coast	the land that is next to the sea
a tour	a trip to an interesting place or around several interesting places
an island	a piece of land that is completely surrounded by water
fit in	to find the time to do something
book	to arrange to have something, such as a hotel room, at a later time
stay on	to remain in a place for more time than you intended

Saying what you have to do

If it is important for you to do something, such as buy a ticket or catch a train, use **I have to ...** or **I need to ...** .

> **I have to** be at the airport at seven.
> **I have to** take the train to Albany first.
> **We have to** be there by 8 o'clock.
> I'm going to get to the station early because **I have to** buy my ticket.

> **I need to** book a bed-and-breakfast.
> **I need to** change trains in Detroit.
> **I need to** call the hotel and book an extra room.
> **We need to** call a taxi.

Useful words

a bed-and-breakfast	a small hotel in which you get a room for the night and a meal in the morning

Saying what you want to do

The simplest way to say that you want to do something such as buy a ticket or take a train is to use **I'd like to ...** . If you know that you do not want to do something, use **I don't want to ...** .

> **I'd like to** rent a bike.
> **I'd like to** make a reservation.
> Good morning, **I'd like to** book a double room.

> **I don't want to** spend too much on a hotel.
> **I don't want to** leave my luggage at the hotel.
> **I don't want to** get stuck in the traffic.

If you are very eager to do something, use **I'd really like to ...** or **I'd love to ...** .

> **I'd really like to** get there early.
> **I'd really like to** come back with Julia.

> **I'd love to** travel as a part of my job.
> **I'd love to** drive across the country.

Use **I'd rather ...** when you want to do one thing and not another. If you want to mention the thing that you do not want, you should use **than**.

> **I'd rather** take the earlier flight.
> **We'd rather** stay in a B&B **than** at a hotel.
> **I'd rather** be near the center of town.

Useful words	
rent	to pay to use something, such as a car, for a short time
a reservation	a room or a table that a hotel or a restaurant keeps for you
a double room	a room in a hotel that is intended for two people
luggage	the bags that you take with you when you travel
stuck	unable to move
traffic	all the vehicles that are on a particular road at one time
B&B	a bed-and-breakfast; a small hotel in which you get a room for the night and a meal in the morning

Making suggestions

The simplest way to make a travel suggestion is to say **We could ...** or **Should we ... ?**

> **We could** take a taxi instead.
> **We could** travel overnight.

> **Should we** walk there?
> **Should we** leave our bags here?

Another way to make a travel suggestion is to say **Why don't ... ?** or **Why not ... ?**

> **Why don't** we hitchhike to the coast?
> **Why don't** you buy a ticket online?

> **Why not** see if Kevin can take us?
> **Why not** ask Aaron if he can drive you to the airport?

Use **How about ... ?** if you have an idea about, for example, where to stay or how to get somewhere.

> **How about** seeing if that bed-and-breakfast downtown has any vacancies?
> **How about** asking Maria to give you a lift?

> **GOOD TO KNOW!**
> **How about + -ing**
> The verb that comes after **How about** must be in the -ing form.

Useful words

overnight	happening through the whole night or at some point during the night
hitchhike	to travel by getting rides from passing vehicles without paying
online	using the Internet
a vacancy	when a room in a hotel is empty
a lift	when you take someone somewhere in your car

Asking for information

You may need to ask if there is a particular place or building where you are traveling. You may need to get someone's attention before you can ask them a question. Use **Excuse me** to do this.

> **Excuse me**, is there a café in the bus station?
> **Excuse me**, is there a subway station near here?
> **Excuse me**, are there any restaurants around here?
> **Excuse me**, are there any ticket booths near here?

Another way to ask this question is **Where can I find ... ?**

> Excuse me, **where can I find** the visitors center?
> Excuse me, **where can I find** information about local bus service?
> Excuse me, **where can I find** the restrooms?

You could use **I'm looking for ...** to get the same information.

> Excuse me, **I'm looking for** the nearest subway station.
> Excuse me, **I'm looking for** the downtown area.
> Excuse me, **I'm looking for** the train station.

You can also ask the same question by starting your sentence with **Do you know ... ?**

> Excuse me, **do you know** where there's a gas station?
> Excuse me, **do you know** where I can find the visitors center?
> Excuse me, **do you know** where the ticket booth is?

Useful words

the subway	a railway system that runs under the ground
a restroom	a public room with toilets for people to use
a gas station	a place where you can buy fuel for your car

If you want someone to suggest something that might be useful to you while you are away, use **Can you recommend ... ?**

>**Can you recommend** a hotel downtown?
>**Can you recommend** a tour guide?

Use **Can you give me the number ... ?** to ask for the phone number of someone who can provide a service for you while you are traveling.

>**Can you give me the number** of a good dentist?
>**Can you give me the number** of a car service?

While you are traveling, you may want to find out the way to do something, for example, how to buy a ticket. Use **How do ... ?**

>Excuse me, **how do** I buy a ticket from this machine?
>**How do** I use this phone?
>**How do** I call a number in Mexico?
>**How do** we get to the station?

Use **Can I ... ?** to ask if you are allowed to do something.

>**Can I** buy a ticket on the train?
>**Can I** leave my bags here?
>**Can I** change my ticket if I need to?
>**Can I** pay by credit card?

If you want to know the time that something happens, ask **What time ... ?**

>**What time** does the train leave?
>**What time** do we get to Rio?
>**What time** do we arrive in Portland?
>**What time** are we boarding?

Useful words

a tour guide	someone who shows tourists around places such as museums or cities
a credit card	a plastic card that you use to buy something and pay for it later
board	to get onto a train, a ship, or an aircraft to travel somewhere

If you want to ask how much time something takes, use **How long ... ?**

> **How long** is the flight?
> **How long** does the trip take?
> **How long** will it take us to walk there?
> **How long** is the subway ride?

If you want to ask how many times something happens, **How often do ... ?**

> **How often do** the trains leave?
> **How often do** the trains to Cambridge leave?
> **How often do** the buses to Oxford leave?

If you want to ask about the money that you need to do something, use **How much ... ?**

> **How much** is a ticket to Beijing?
> **How much** is a round-trip ticket?
> **How much** does it cost to fly there?
> **How much** does it cost to rent a car?

Asking for things

If you want to ask for something while you are traveling, the simplest way is to use **Can I have ... ?** or **Could I have ... ?** To be very polite, use **please**.

> **Can I have** an aisle seat, please?
> Please **can I have** a timetable?

Useful words

a trip	a short journey that you make to a particular place
a round-trip ticket	a ticket for a journey to a place and back again
an aisle	a long, narrow passage where people can walk between rows of seats
a timetable	a list of the times when trains, buses, or planes arrive and depart

Could I have a ticket to Palm Beach, please?
Could I have a weekly pass, please?

If you want to find out if something is available, use **Do you have … ?**

Excuse me, **do you have** a lost-and-found?
Excuse me, **do you have** a non-smoking area?

If you are asking someone whether they can do something for you, use
Can you … ? or **Could you … ? Could you … ?** is slightly more formal than
Can you … ? To be polite, use **please**.

Can you please help me?
Can you let me out here, **please**?

Could you give me directions downtown, **please**?
Could you write down the address for me, **please**?

A very polite way to ask someone if they will do something for you is **Would
you mind … ?** or **Do you mind … ?**

Would you mind writing down the address for me?
Would you mind dropping me off at my hotel?

Do you mind showing me where the hotel is on this map?
Do you mind looking after my bag, please?

Useful words

weekly	for one week, or happening every week
a pass	a document that allows you to do something
a lost-and-found office	a place where things that people have lost are stored
non-smoking	where smoking is not allowed
directions	instructions that tell you how to get somewhere
write something down	to record something on a piece of paper using a pen or a pencil
drop off	to take someone somewhere in a car and leave them there
look after someone/ something	to take care of someone or something

> **GOOD TO KNOW!**
> **Would/Do you mind + -ing**
> The verb that comes after **Would/Do you mind ... ?** must be in the -ing form.

Use **Could I ... ?** or **May I ... ?** when you want to ask if you can do something.

Could I get my luggage, please?
Could I check in, please?
Could I leave my bags here, please?

May I see the receipt?
May I sit here?
May I put my bag here?

Saying what you like, dislike, prefer

You may want to talk about what you like and do not like about traveling. The simplest way to say that you like something is to use **I like ...** . To say that you like doing an activity, use **I enjoy ...** . To ask someone if they like or enjoy something, use **Do you like ... ?** or **Do you enjoy ... ?**

I like traveling on the the high-speed trains.
Do you like driving or being driven?

I enjoy just looking out of the window.
Do you enjoy exploring new places?

Useful words

check in	to tell the person at an airport or a hotel that you have arrived
high-speed	fast
explore	to travel around a place to find out what it is like

If you want to say that you like something very much, use **I really like ...** or **I love ...** .

> **I really like** these country roads.
> **I really like** traveling because you get to see a different way of life.

> **I love** looking at the scenery from the train.
> I'm very happy when I'm traveling but I also **love** coming home.

To say that you do not like something, use **I don't like ...** , or to say that you *really* do not like something, use **I hate ...** .

> **I don't like** flying.
> **I don't like** carrying a backpack.

> **I hate** getting stuck in traffic.
> **I hate** long-distance flights.

If you want to say that you like one thing more than another thing, use **I prefer ...** . To talk about the thing that you like less, use **to**.

> **I prefer** taking the train **to** driving.
> I sometimes travel on my own, but **I prefer** traveling with other people.

Useful words

scenery	the natural surroundings that you can see around you
a backpack	a bag that you carry on your back
a long-distance flight	a flight over a long distance

● Listen for

Here are some important phrases you are likely to hear and use when you are traveling.

Could I see your tickets, please?
Could you have your tickets ready, please?
This is the 5:45 to London, stopping at Finsbury Park only.
A round-trip ticket to Portland, please.
A one-way ticket to Seoul, please.
Change at Times Square.
The train for Vancouver leaves from Platform Three.
Do you mind if I sit here?
Passengers are reminded to take all their personal belongings with them when they leave the train.

Flight 208 is now boarding at Gate 12.
Passengers are reminded that smoking is not allowed anywhere on the plane.
Please store all bags in the overhead bins.

Go straight on until you get to the traffic lights.
Continue down this road.
Take the second turn on the left.
It's opposite the cathedral.
You can walk there.
It's too far to walk.
It will take you ten minutes to walk there.
It's three stops from here.

Useful words

Do you mind ... ?	used to ask someone if you can do something
remind	to say something that makes someone remember something
belongings	the things that you own
overhead	above you
a bin	a container that you keep things in
straight on	continuing in one direction
continue	to start again after stopping

Listen to the conversation: Track 3

Emma is telling her colleague Jim about her travel plans.

A So what are your plans for this summer?

B I've decided I'm going to travel with my friend, Ashley.

A Really, where are you going?

B We're thinking we'd like to travel around southern California — Santa Barbara and San Diego, and we're hoping to get to Monterrey, too.

A How are you going to get there?

B Well, we both hate flying, so we're planning to take the train.

A Really? I'd always rather fly. It's so much quicker and more convenient.

B Not me, I prefer trains and boats — they're so much more relaxing. I like sitting back and enjoying the scenery.

A Do you think you'll get to the Channel Islands?

B I hope so. Have you been there?

A Yes, I worked there last summer — it's a great national park. You really should go there.

B Well, we'll make sure we go then! Do you have a travel guide for the park, by any chance?

A I do — a good one.

B Would you mind lending it to me?

A Sure. I'll bring it the next time we get together.

B And what about you? Are you going to get away this summer?

A I don't know — work is going to be very busy over the next few months.
I might manage a weekend somewhere – maybe Cape Cod.
I'll have to see how it goes.

B You like the Cape, don't you?

A Very much. I really like the way of life there. I sometimes think I'd like
to live there. Anyway, I'd better go now. I'm supposed to meet Enrique
in ten minutes.

B OK, bye!

A Bye, Emma!

> ## Listen to more phrases and practice saying them: Track 4

Where we live

Make yourself at home!

The phrases in this unit will help you to talk about your accommodations.
You can use them if you are trying to find a hotel, if you are looking for
somewhere to live, or if you want to talk about the place where you live.

Asking for things

To say what kind of place you want to live in, either a hotel or a place to rent or
buy, use **I'd like ...** .

> **I'd like** a double room.
> **I'd like** to rent a cabin in the mountains.
> **I'd like** a ground floor apartment.
> **I'd like** room with a view.

To talk about the kind of place you want, use **I'm looking for ...** .

> **I'm looking for** a room in a house.
> **I'm looking for** a cheap place to stay.
> **I'm looking for** a place to rent.
> **We're looking for** a house with four bedrooms and a garage.

> **GOOD TO KNOW!**
> **Accommodations** is one of the words most often spelled wrong in
> American English. Remember that it has **cc** and **mm**.

Useful words

accommodations	buildings or rooms where people live or stay
a double room	a room for two people
rent	to pay the owner of something in order to be able to use it yourself
a cabin	a small wooden house in the woods or mountains
the ground floor	the part of a building that is at the same level as the ground
the view	everything you can see from a place
a garage	a building where you keep a car

To explain to someone what you want, use **I want ...** .

> **I want** a house with a large garden.
> **I want** to rent a house for six months.
> **I wanted** a bigger kitchen.
> **We don't want** to live in the suburbs.

If you are in a hotel, and you need something, use **Could I have ... ?**

> **Could I have** the key to my room, please?
> **Could I have** a receipt, please?
> **Could I have** an extra pillow, please?
> **Could we have** some more towels?

To make sure that a hotel has everything you need, use **Do you have ... ?**

> **Do you have** Internet access?
> **Do you have** a gym?
> **Do you have** an indoor pool?
> **Do you have** conference facilities?

To ask someone to do something for you, use **Could you ... ?**

> **Could you** ask the landlord to fix the heating?
> **Could you** let me know if any similar houses come on the market?
> **Could you** call a taxi for me, please?
> **Could you** tell me how far it is from the station?

Useful words

a suburb	one of the areas on the edge of a city where many people live
a receipt	a piece of paper that shows that you have paid for something
a pillow	a soft object that you rest your head on when you are in bed
access	when you are able to use equipment
a gym	a club, a building, or a large room with equipment for doing physical exercises
a conference	a long meeting about a particular subject
facilities	a room, a building, or a piece of equipment that used for a particular purpose
a landlord	a man who owns a building and allows people to live there in return for rent

Asking for information

When you want to obtain some information about your accommodations, the simplest way is to start your question with **Is ... ?**

> **Is** it near the university?
> **Is** it a luxury hotel?
> **Is** the apartment available immediately?
> **Is** breakfast included?
> **Are** utilities included in the rent?

You could also use **Could you tell me ... ?** or **I'd like to know ...** .

> **Could you tell me** what the neighborhood is like?
> **Could you tell me** if there is a laundry room?
> **Could you tell me** what the rent is?

> **I'd like to know** if the hotel has a swimming pool.
> **I'd like to know** how much a double room would be.
> **I'd like to know** whether you have any three-bedroom houses to rent.

To ask if a place has something, use **Is there ... ?** or **Does ... have ... ?**

> **Is there** an ironing board in the room?
> **Is there** hair dryer?
> **Are there** any pillows in the closet?
> **Are there** any rules about having guests?

Useful words

luxury	being pleasant and expensive
a neighborhood	one of the parts of a town where people live
laundry	clothes and other things that need to be washed
an ironing board	a narrow surface like a table that you use for ironing

Does the apartment **have** central heating?
Does the hotel **have** a gym?
Does it **have** a deck?
Does it **have** a garage?

To ask what something is like, use **What's ... like?**

What are your accommodations **like**?
What's the area **like** for shopping?
What's the mattress **like** on your bed?

Use **Where ... ?** to ask about where things are.

Where's the laundry room?
Where's the nearest train station?
Where can I plug my laptop in?

To ask about time, use **What time ... ?**

What time's breakfast?
What time is the real estate agent coming?
What time do we have to leave in the morning?

To ask about prices, use **How much ... ?**

How much is a family room?
How much do you pay your cleaning service?
How much do you charge for breakfast?

Useful words

central heating	a heating system that uses hot air or water to heat every part of a building
a deck	a flat wooden area attached to a house, where people can sit
plug something in	to connect a piece of electrical equipment to the electricity supply
a real estate agent	a person whose job is to sell buildings or land

If you want to ask someone's advice about your accommodations, use **Can you give me some advice ... ?** Use the prepositions **about** or **on** after this phrase.

> **Can you give me some advice about** how to choose a real estate agent?
> **Can you give me some advice on** the best areas to look for an apartment?
> **Can you give me some advice about** having roommates?

To ask someone about the best thing to do, use **Would you recommend ... ?**

> **Would you recommend** hiring a builder to do the work?
> **Would you recommend** buying my own place?
> **Would you recommend** that hotel?

> **GOOD TO KNOW!**
> **Would you recommend + -ing verb**
> When **Would you recommend** is followed by a verb, it must be in the
> -ing form.

Asking for permission

If you are staying in a hotel or renting somewhere to live, you may need to ask for permission. You can use **Can I ... .**

> **Can I** park outside?
> **Can I** leave my suitcases here for five minutes?
> **Can we** use the pool?
> **Can we** camp here?
> **Can we** stay another night?
> **Can we** have pets?

Useful words	
a roommate	someone who you share a house or an apartment with
camp	to stay somewhere in a tent
a pet	an animal that you keep in your home

To check if something is allowed or permitted, use **Can I ... ?**

> **Can I** use the washing machine?
> **Can I** have guests?
> **Can we** bring our dog?

To make sure you will not upset someone, use **Do you mind if ... ?**

> **Do you mind if** I keep my bike in the garage?
> **Do you mind if** I use the washing machine?
> **Do you mind if** we have a party this weekend?

You can also use **Is it OK to ... ?** This is informal.

> **Is it OK to** bring some of my own furniture?
> **Is it OK to** turn the heat on?
> **Is it OK to** paint my room?

Saying what you like, dislike, prefer

When you are looking for accommodations, you will probaby need to explain what you like or do not like. The simplest phrase to use is **I like ...** .

> **I like** modern architecture.
> I really **like** camping in the mountains.
> **I like** living in the country.
> **I don't like** this wallpaper.
> **We don't like** living in an apartment.

Useful words

architecture	the style of the design of a building
camp	to stay in a tent
wallpaper	colored or patterned paper that is used for decorating walls

If you want to say that you like one thing more than another, use **I prefer ...** .
If you want to talk about the thing you like less, use **to**.

>**I prefer** wood floors to carpets.
>**I prefer** buying a place to renting.
>**I prefer** living on my own.
>**I prefer** blinds to curtains.

To say what you would prefer to do, use **I'd rather ...** . If you want to talk about
the thing you would not like to do, use **than**.

>**I'd rather** use a cleaning service.
>**I'd rather** have a roommate **than** live on my own.
>**We'd rather** have the loft converted **than** move to another house.

If you would prefer not to do something, use **I'd prefer not to ...** or **I'd rather
not ...** .

>**I'd prefer not to** have a roommate.
>**I'd prefer not to** stay in a hotel.
>**I'd prefer not to** spend too much money.

>**I'd rather not** live too far from work.
>**I'd rather not** have to do much decorating.
>**I'd rather not** have roommates.

> **GOOD TO KNOW!**
> **I'd rather not + infinitive**
> The verb that follows **I'd rather not** must be in the base form.

Useful words

a blind	a piece of cloth or other material that you can pull down over a window to cover it
a loft	the space directly under the roof of a building
convert	to change something into a different form
decorate	to put new paint or paper on the walls or ceiling of a room

Talking about your plans

If you have decided what you are going to do, you could use **I'm going to ...** or **I'm planning to ...** .

> **I'm going to** buy a house closer to work.
> **I'm going to** stay in a hotel while the construction work is going on.
> **We're going to** go camping.

> **I'm planning to** get an architect to design the extension.
> **I'm planning to** paint the walls yellow.
> **I'm planning to** have roommates.

You can also use **I'll ...** to say what you are going to do.

> **I'll** be at the hotel at five p.m.
> **I'll** probably rent at first.
> **We'll** be there by seven.

To talk about something that you would like to do but are not sure is possible, use **I'm hoping to ...** .

> **I'm hoping to** find an apartment with a spare bedroom.
> **I'm hoping to** move to Nevada in the spring.
> **I'm hoping to** find someone to share a house with.

Useful words
an architect   a person whose job is to design buildings
an extension   an extra part that is added to a building to make it bigger

Complaining

Unfortunately, you may need to complain to the hotel staff or to your landlord or landlady. To talk about something that is upsetting you, use **There's ...**, and for something you think is missing, use **There isn't ...** .

> **There's** mold in the bathroom.
> **There's** a leak in the ceiling.
> **There are** mice.

> **There isn't** any hot water.
> **There aren't** any curtains.
> **There aren't** any clean towels in the room.

If something is not good enough, use **I'm not happy with ...** or **I'm disappointed with ...** .

> **I'm not happy with** the parking arrangements.
> **I'm not happy with** the food.
> **I'm not happy with** my room.

> **I'm disappointed with** the view.
> **I'm disappointed with** the food.
> **I'm disappointed with** the neighborhood.

To say that you think something is bad, use **I think ...** .

> **I think** the beds are really uncomfortable.
> **I think** the rooms are cold and drafty.
> **I don't think** the rooms are cleaned often enough.

Useful words

mold	a soft grey or green substance that grows on old food or damp surfaces
a leak	when liquid or gas escapes from something
drafty	having streams of cold air

● Listen for

Here are some useful phrases you may hear when you are finding somewhere to stay or live.

What type of accommodations are you looking for?
Whose name is the reservation in?
For how many nights?
For how many people?
Breakfast is included.
Can I see your passport, please?
I'm afraid we're full.
We still have a few vacancies.
There's a 300-dollar deposit.
You need to give two months' notice when you want to leave.
What number can we contact you at?
We don't allow dogs.
How would you like to pay?
Please fill out this form.
Please sign here.
Can you spell your name for me, please?
Would you like a wake-up call?
How would you like to pay?

Useful words

a reservation	an arrangement to have a hotel or a restaurant to keep a room or table for you
a deposit	a sum of money that you give as part of the payment for goods or services
notice	a warning that something will happen
a vacancy	a room that is still available
a wake-up call	a telephone call to wake you up in the morning

Listen to the conversation: Track 5

Emma and Brett have met for lunch. Emma is explaining why she wants to move out of her apartment.

A I'm trying to find a new apartment, closer to work. I'm not happy with the place where I am at the moment.

B Why not? Isn't it nice?

A Not really. It's very expensive and kind of small. It doesn't have a spare bedroom, so if I have guests, they have to sleep on the sofa. Also, there's no washing machine, and the refrigerator and stove are very old and don't work very well.

B So have you started looking?

A Yeah. I have to give my landlord a month's notice, so I'm hoping to find a place soon. I'm trying to decide which area to go for — would you recommend living downtown?

B Well, I love it because I go out a lot, but it's kind of noisy. It depends on what's important to you.

A I'd probably prefer somewhere quieter, but I'd like to be near downtown.

B I'm sure you could find something nice nearby. I've got a friend who lives near the river. Would you like to talk to her about what it's like there?

A That would be great. I've been thinking about looking there.

 Listen to more phrases and practice saying them: Track 6

Eating with friends

Enjoy your meal!

If you are going out for a meal, you will need to make arrangements with your friends about when and where to meet. You will also want to order food and perhaps tell your friends what food you like and do not like. The phrases in this unit will help you to do all this with confidence.

Making arrangements

When you make arrangements with people, you may want to check if they are happy with the plan. Use **How would you feel about ... ?**

> **How would you feel about** having dinner in town?
> **How would you feel about** meeting at the restaurant?
> **How would you feel about** eating earlier?

To ask people if they would prefer a different arrangement, use **Would you prefer it if ... ?** or **Would it be better ... ?**

> **Would you prefer it if** we went to the Italian restaurant near you?
> **Would you prefer it if** we didn't invite Claudia?
> **Would you prefer it if** we postponed dinner until next week?

> **Would it be better** to reserve a table in advance?
> **Would it be better** to go to a restaurant that we know?
> **Would it be better** if we ate out somewhere?

To make sure someone is happy with a plan, use **Is ... OK?**

> **Is** seven o'clock for dinner **OK** with you?
> I was thinking of the Greek restaurant on South Main Street. **Is** that **OK** with you?

Useful words

postpone	to arrange for an event to happen at a later time
reserve	to arrange to have a hotel or a restaurant to keep a room or a table for you
in advance	before a particular date or event
eat out	to eat in a restaurant

Is it **OK** if I get to the restaurant later?
Is it **OK** to meet in the restaurant?

Another way to make sure that someone is happy with a plan is to use **How does ... sound?**

I was thinking we'd meet for dinner and then see a movie. **How does** that **sound?**
What about dinner at 8:00 at Franco's? **How does** that **sound** to you?
What about a snack in The Book Shop Café, followed by shopping? **How does** that **sound?**
How does eight-thirty for dinner **sound?**

Asking for information

Use **Is ... ?** to ask general questions about the food that is on the menu.

Is the pasta dish vegetarian?
Is the sauce hot?

Useful words

a snack	a simple meal that is quick to prepare and to eat
a menu	a list of the food and drink that you can have in a restaurant
pasta	a type of food made from a mixture of flour, eggs, and water that is made into different shapes
vegetarian	not containing meat or fish
sauce	a thick liquid that you eat with other food.
hot	having a strong burning taste

Is this dish spicy?
Is that a type of meat?

Use **What is ... ?** to ask about a particular dish.

What is "gravy"?
What is "jelly"?
What is that on your plate?

Use **What's in ... ?** to ask about the foods that are in a particular dish.

What's in this dish?
What's in a "cassoulet"?
Can I ask **what's in** this dish?

Use **Is there any ... ?** or **Are there any ... ?** to ask whether a particular food is in a dish.

Is there any milk in this?
Is there any alcohol in this?
Are there any nuts in this dish?
Are there any bones in the fish?

Useful words

spicy	strongly flavored with spices
gravy	a sauce made from the juices that come from meat when it cooks
jelly	a sweet food that contains soft fruit and sugar
alcohol	a liquid that is found in drinks such as beer and wine
a nut	a dry fruit with a hard shell
a bone	one of the hard white parts inside a person's or animal's body

Asking for things

When you arrive at the restaurant, you will want to tell the waiter or waitress how many people will be eating so he can find the right sized table for you. Use **A table for ... please**.

> **A table for** two, **please**.
> "**A table for** six, **please**." "Certainly, sir. Come this way."

In most restaurants someone will soon come to your table to take your order. To say which dish you want, use **I'd like ...** or **I'll have ...** . To be very polite, use **please**.

> **I'd like** the Margarita pizza, please.
> For my appetizer, **I'd like** the salad, please.
> For my main course, **I'd like** the pasta.
> For dessert, **I'd like** ice cream.

> **I'll have** the lamb, please.
> **I'll have** the fish soup as an appetizer, please.
> For dessert, **I'll have** the fruit.
> **We'll have** water to drink.

> **GOOD TO KNOW!**
> If the waiter or waitress comes to your table to take your order, and you have not decided what to choose, say **We haven't decided yet** or **Could you come back in a few minutes, please?**

Useful words

an order	the thing that someone has asked for
an appetizer	a small amount of food that you eat as the first part of a meal
a salad	a mixture of food, usually vegetables, that you usually serve cold
a main course	the biggest part of a meal
a dessert	something sweet that you eat at the end of a meal
lamb	the flesh of a lamb, eaten as food
soup	a liquid food made by boiling meat, fish, or vegetables in water

To ask if something is available, use **Do you have ... ?**

> **Do you have** a children's menu?
> **Do you have** a table outside?

If the waiter or waitress has brought food to your table, but you need something else, use **Can I have ... ?** or **Could I have ... ?** To be very polite, use **please**.

> **Can I have** the dessert menu, please?
> **Can I** please **have** some pepper?
> **Can I have** some ketchup, please?

> **Can I** please **have** another fork?
> **Could I have** some water, please?
> **Could I have** the bill, please?

If you are asking someone if they can do something for you, use **Can you ... ?** or **Could you ... ? Could you ... ?** is slightly more polite and formal than **Can you ... ?**

> **Can you** pass me the salt, please?
> **Can you** please bring us another glass?

> **Could you** bring us our coffee, please?
> **Could you** bring us the bill, please?

Useful words

pepper	a spice with a hot taste that you put on food
ketchup	a thick red sauce made from tomatoes
a fork	a tool with long metal points used for eating food
pass	to give an object to someone
the bill	a piece of paper that shows how much money you must pay for something

A polite way of asking someone to do something is by asking **Would you mind … ?**

> **Would you mind** taking our order?
> **Would you mind** bringing us some salt?

To ask whether something you want is possible, use **Is it possible to … ?**

> **Is it possible to** change our order?
> **Is it possible to** have the soup for my main course?

Saying what you want to do

To say what you want to do, use **I'd like to … .** If you are very eager to do something, use **I'd really like to …** or **I'd love to … .**

> **I'd like to** eat a little earlier.
> **I'd like to** have fish tonight.

> **I'd really like to** try that new Spanish restaurant on Green Street.
> **I'd really like to** eat there again.

> **I'd love to** have dessert.
> **I'd love to** take Carlos to that restaurant.

Use **I'd rather …** when you want to do one thing more than another. If you want to mention the thing that you do not want, use **than**.

> **I'd rather** eat later, if that's possible.
> **I'd rather** eat in the hotel **than** go out to a restaurant.

Useful words

salt   a white substance that you use to improve the flavor of food

Saying what you like, dislike, prefer

When you are eating in a restaurant, you may like to talk about the food that you like and do not like. The simplest way to talk about things you like is to use **I like ...** . To talk about activities that you like doing, use **I enjoy ...** .

> **I like** all kinds of cheese.
> **I like** most vegetables.
> **Do you like** spicy food?

> **I enjoy** eating out with friends.
> I really **enjoy** going to new restaurants.
> **Do you enjoy** trying different kinds of food?

> **GOOD TO KNOW!**
> **Like/Enjoy + -ing**
> When **like** or **enjoy** is followed by a verb, the verb is usually in the -ing form.

If you like something, but not in a strong way, use **I sort of like ...** .

> **I sort of like** ice cream.
> **I sort of like** hamburgers.

If you like something very much, you can say **I really like ...** or **I love ...** .

> **I really like** Indian food.
> **I really like** meat.

> **I love** seafood.
> **I love** dessert.

Useful words

spicy	strongly flavored with spices
a hamburger	meat that is pressed into a flat, round shape, eaten between two pieces of bread
seafood	fish and other small animals from the ocean that you can eat

To tell someone that you do not like a food, use **I don't like ...** .

>**I don't like** olives.
>**I don't like** fast food.

To confirm that something is true, use **Don't you like ... ?**

>**Don't you like** sweet food?
>**Don't you like** chocolate?

To say very strongly that you do not like a food, use **I hate ...** .

>**I hate** mushrooms.
>**She hates** tomatoes.

If you want to say that you like one food more than another, use **I prefer ...** .
If you want to talk about the food you don't like as much, use **to**.

>I don't really like meat. **I prefer** fish.
>**I prefer** eating at home **to** eating at a restaurant.

To talk about something that you do not like to do, use **I prefer not to ...** .

>**I prefer not to** eat late at night.
>**She prefers not to** eat a lot of rich food.

Useful words

an olive	a small green or black fruit with a bitter taste
fast food	hot food that is served quickly in a restaurant
a mushroom	a plant with a short stem and a round part that you can eat
rich	containing a lot of butter, eggs, or cream

Asking for suggestions

If you want to ask the waiter or the people at your table to tell you about something good to eat, use **Can you recommend ... ?** or **What do you recommend ... ?**

> **Can you recommend** a drink to go with our meal?
> **Can you recommend** a local dish?
> **Can you recommend** a specialty of the region?

> **What do you recommend** for an appetizer?
> **What do you recommend** for dessert?
> You've been to this restaurant before, Pilar. **What do you recommend?**

To give you an idea about what to eat, you might ask someone at your table what they have chosen. Use **What are you having ... ?**

> **What are you having**, Juan?
> **What are you having** for dessert, Yuta?
> **What are you having** for your appetizer?

If you want to ask whether you should have or do something, use **Do you think I should ... ?**

> **Do you think I should** have the pie?
> **Do you think I should** try the snails?
> **Do you think we should** leave a larger tip?

Useful words

local	in or relating to the area where you live
a specialty	a special food or product that is always very good in a particular place
a region	an area of the country or of the world
a pie	a dish of fruit, meat, or vegetables that is covered with pastry (= a mixture of flour, butter, and water) and baked
a snail	a small animal with a long, soft body, no legs, and a shell on its back
a tip	money that you give to someone to thank them for a job that they have done for you

Making suggestions

The simplest way to make a suggestion is to use **We could ...** .

>**We could** eat here, if you like.
>**We could** just have a salad.

If you want to make a suggestion and see if other people agree with you, use **Should we ... ?**

>**Should we** order?
>**Should we** see what that new French restaurant is like?

If you have an idea about something, use **How about ... ?**

>**How about** finding somewhere in town to eat?
>**How about** sharing a dessert?

Another way to make a suggestion is to say **Why don't ... ?**

>**Why don't** we ask Neil to join us?
>**Why don't** you walk to the restaurant and take a taxi home?

I suggest ... is a stronger way of making a suggestion.

>**I suggest** you take a taxi to the restaurant.
>**I suggest** we order a variety of dishes and then share them.

> **GOOD TO KNOW!**
> The verb that follows **I suggest** should be in the simple present tense.

Useful words

share	to have or use something with another person
a variety	a number of things that are different from each other

Talking about your plans

To say what you have decided to eat, use **I'm having the ...** or **I'm going to have the ...** .

> **I'm having the** pie.
> **I'm having the** soup for my appetizer.
>
> **I'm going to have the** fish stew.
> **I'm going to have the** pasta for my main course.

If you do not know what to choose, use **I can't decide what to have ...** .

> **I can't decide what to have** for an appetizer.
> **I can't decide what to have** for a main course.
> There are so many delicious things. **I can't decide what to have**.

If you think you might choose something, use **Maybe I'll have the ...** .

> **Maybe I'll have the** salad.
> **Maybe I'll have the** salmon for my main course.

If you change your decision about what you are going to eat, use **I've changed my mind ...** .

> **I've changed my mind** — I'm having the lamb.
> **I've changed my mind** — I'm not having dessert.
> **She's changed her mind** — she's going to have the soup for her starter.

Useful words

a stew	a meal that you make by cooking meat and vegetables in water
delicious	very good to eat
salmon	the pink flesh of a large fish with silver skin

• Listen for

Here are some useful phrases you may hear in a restaurant.

> Do you have a reservation?
> I'm sorry. We're full.
> This way, please.
> Follow me, please.
> Smoking or non-smoking?
> Here's the menu.
> Would you like to see the dessert menu?
> Can I take your order?
> And for you, sir?
> And for you, madam?
> Today's specials are on the board.
> I'd recommend the fish tacos.
> Are you ready to order?
> The pasta comes with a green salad.
> Would you like to start with an appetizer?
> What will you have to drink?
> Can I get you something to drink?
> Would you like anything else?
> Can I get you anything else?
> Is that everything?
> Is everything all right?
> I'll be right with you.
> I'll bring it right away.

Useful words

full	containing as many people as possible
a special	a dish in a restaurant that is available only on a particular day and is not usually available
taco	a crispy Mexican pancake made from corn and eggs, which is folded and filled with meat, vegetables, and a spicy sauce
right away	immediately

Listen to the conversation: Track 7

Emma and her friend Ashley are making arrangements to go out to dinner.

A I'd really like to try that new Mexican restaurant next to Walker's on Main Street.

B Me, too. Let's go there.

A Great. Should we invite Miyoko? I haven't seen her in ages.

B Yeah, good idea — I'd love to see her.

A Could you call her? I don't have her number.

B Sure. Should we reserve a table?

A Yeah, we probably should — it's pretty popular.

B What time do you want to meet?

A How does seven o'clock sound?

B Would you mind if we met a little later — seven-thirty, say? I don't get out of work until six o'clock on Thursdays and I don't think I can get there by seven.

A Of course. That'll be fine.

B By the way, how are you planning to get there?

A I'm not sure. I might walk.

B Would you prefer it if I drove you? I could pick you up at around seven, if you like.

A That would be great.

B Perfect. See you at seven o'clock tonight, hopefully with Miyoko.

A See you then!

 Listen to more phrases and practice saying them: Track 8

Going out

Have a good time!

If you are going out, whether it is to a party, a concert, or the movies, these phrases will help you say what you want, ask where things are, and ask for what you need.

Making suggestions

One easy way of making a suggestion about where to go and what to do, is to use **We could ...** .

> **We could** go and see a movie.
> **We could** go to a club, if you like.
> **We could** go to the theater, if you like.

> **GOOD TO KNOW!**
> When people start a sentence with **We could ...** they often add **if you like** at the end.

If you are eager to do something with someone, use **Let's ...** .

> **Let's** go to the movies.
> **Let's** buy tickets for Saturday's game.
> I've got a good idea. **Let's** all go swimming.

Another way to make a suggestion about where to go and what to do is to use **Should we ... ?**

> **Should we** go out for dinner?
> **Should we** have a barbecue and invite some friends?
> **Should we** go out for a walk?

Useful words

a game	an activity or a sport in which you try to win against someone
a barbecue	a party where you cook food on a piece of equipment outdoors

If you have an idea about what to do or where to go, use **How about ... ?** or
What about ... ?

> **How about** going somewhere for coffee?
> **How about** going bowling?
>
> **What about** going somewhere where we can listen to some good music?
> **What about** going on a picnic?

> **GOOD TO KNOW!**
> **How about/What about + -ing**
> A verb that comes after **How about** or **What about** must be in the
> -ing form.

To suggest what someone else can do or where someone else can go, use
You could ... .

> **You could** go to a concert.
> After your meal, **you could** have ice cream on the deck.

You can also use **Why not ... ?** or **Why don't ... ?** if you have an idea about what
someone else might do.

> **Why not** invite some friends from work?
> If you don't have anything to do, **why not** go to Jake's party?

> **Why don't** we have a party for him?
> **Why don't** you come to the party after the movie?

Useful words

bowling	a game in which you roll a heavy ball down a narrow track toward a group of wooden objects and try to knock them down
a picnic	a meal that is eaten outdoors
a concert	a performance of music
a deck	a flat wooden area attached to a house, where people can sit

I suggest ... and **You should ...** are slightly strong ways of making a suggestion.

> **I suggest** we take a taxi there.
> **You should** invite her husband, too.

Talking about your plans

The simplest way of talking about a plan that you are sure of is to use **I'm** followed by a verb in the **-ing** form.

> **I'm seeing** Julio and Sasha tonight.
> **We're having** a party for Pia on Saturday.

The simplest way of asking someone what they plan to do is **What are you going to do...?** or **What are you doing ... ?**

> **What are you going to do** tonight?
> **What are you doing** for your birthday?

For a plan that you are sure of, you can also use **I'm going to ...** . Use **Are you going to ... ?** to ask someone if they will do something.

> **I'm going to** go out with some friends tonight.
> **We're going to** have dinner at our friends' house tonight.

> **Are you going to** celebrate?
> **Are you going to** invite many people?

Useful words
go out   to leave your home to do something enjoyable
celebrate   to do something enjoyable for a special reason

You can use **I'm planning to ...** or **I plan to ...**, for something that you want to do, but which is not certain.

> **I'm planning to** invite my neighbors.
> **We're planning to** drop by on our way home.

> **I plan to** take her out for dinner while I'm in New York.
> **I plan to** have some friends over for my birthday.

To talk about something that you would like to do but are not sure that you will do, you can use **I'm hoping to ...** or **I hope to ...** .

> **I'm hoping to** see them in concert.
> **He's hoping to** go to the theater while he's there.

> **I hope to** visit Marrakech while I'm in Morocco.
> **We hope to** go to the ballet while we're in Moscow.

To talk about a plan that is only possible, use **I might ...** .

> **I might** see a band this weekend.
> **I might** meet up with Farida and Saki tonight.
> **We might** go to a club afterwards.

To talk about what should happen in the future, use **I'm supposed to ...** .

> **I'm supposed to** be at the restaurant at eight o'clock.
> **I'm supposed to** be home in half an hour.

Useful words

a neighbor	someone who lives near you
drop by	to visit someone
take someone out	to take someone somewhere enjoyable
ballet	a type of dancing that needs a lot of skill and in which there are carefully planned movements
a band	a group of people who play music together
meet up	to come together with people

Asking for information

Use **Is ... ?** to ask general questions requiring information.

>**Is** the club generally busy on Friday night?
>**Is** the club open on Sunday?
>**Is** it expensive to go to the ballet?

Use **Is there ... ?** or **Do you have ... ?** to ask whether something exists.

>Excuse me, **is there** a bookstore in this part of town?
>**Is there** a football game on this afternoon?
>Excuse me, **are there** any free concerts this weekend?

>**Do you have** any tickets left?
>**Do you have** any tickets for tonight's performance?
>**Do you have** any programs?

If you want to know the time that something happens, use **What time ... ?**

>**What time** does the movie start?
>**What time** does the concert finish?
>**What time** do you want to meet?

To ask how much time something lasts for, use **How long ... ?**

>**How long** is the movie?
>**How long** is the concert?
>**How long** will you be there?

Useful words

busy	full of people who are doing things
left	still there after everything else has gone or been used
a performance	when you entertain an audience by singing, dancing, or acting
a program	a small book or sheet of paper that tells you about a play or concert

If you want to ask about the money that you need to do something, use **How much ... ?**

> **How much** is it to get in?
> **How much** is a ticket?
> **How much** does it cost to watch the match?

To ask how to do something, use **How do you ... ?**

> **How do you** get tickets?
> **How do you** turn this on?
> **How do you** get to the center of town?

Asking for things

To ask for something, use **Can I have ... ?** or **Could I have ... ?** To be very polite, use please.

> **Can I have** two tickets for the show, please?
> **Can I have** a concert program, please?

> **Could I have** a cup of coffee, please?
> **Could I have** some more?

Another way of asking for something is **I'd like ...** .

> **I'd like** a glass of orange juice, please.
> **I'd like** a ticket for tonight's game.
> **I'd like** three tickets, please.

Useful words
a show   a performance in a theater
juice   the liquid from a fruit or a vegetable

If you are asking someone if they can do something for you, use **Can you ... ?**
or **Could you ... ? Could you ... ?** is slightly more polite and formal than
Can you... ? To be very polite, use **please**.

> **Can you** tell me where the entrance is, please?
> **Can you** find our seats while I buy our drinks?

> **Could you** take me to Jewels, please.
> **Could you** get me a drink, please?

Saying what you like, dislike, prefer

To talk about things you like, use **I like ...** and to ask someone if they like
something, ask **Do you like ... ?**

> **I like** listening to live music.
> **I like** going out with my friends.
> **He likes** dance music.

> **Do you like** dancing?
> **Do you like** horror movies?
> **Do you like** eating out?

> **GOOD TO KNOW!**
> **like + -ing**
> When **like** is followed by a verb, the verb is usually in the -ing form.

If you like something, but not in a strong way, use **I sort of like ...** .

> **I sort of like** going to the movies.
> **I sort of like** the theater.
> **I sort of like** going out at night, but I prefer staying in.

Useful words

entrance	the door or gate where you go into a place
a horror movie	a very frightening movie that you watch for entertainment
eat out	to eat in a restaurant
stay in	to remain at home and not go out

If you like something very much, you can say **I really like ...** or **I love ...** .

> **I really like** going on picnics in the summer.
> **I really like** going to the opera.
> **I really like** live music.

> **I love** having dinner with my friends.
> **I love** taking taxis.
> I absolutely **love** musicals.

To tell someone what you do not like, use **I don't like ...** .

> **I don't like** football.
> **I don't like** going to the theater.
> **I don't** really **like** science fiction movies.

A slightly formal way of saying what you don't like is **I dislike ...** .

> **I dislike** having to stand in line to get in.
> **I dislike** paying restaurant prices.
> **He dislikes** noisy places.

To say very strongly that you do not like something, use **I hate ...** .

> **I hate** opera.
> **I hate** being in a crowd.
> I absolutely **hate** noisy clubs.

Useful words

opera	a play with music in which all the words are sung
live music	music that is performed before an audience
a musical	a play or a film that uses singing or dancing in the story
science fiction	stories about life in the future or in other parts of the universe
noisy	making a lot of loud or unpleasant noise
a crowd	a large group of people who have gathered together

> **GOOD TO KNOW!**
> **Hate + -ing**
> When **hate** is followed by a verb, the verb is usually in the -ing form.

If you want to say that you like one thing more than another, use **I prefer ...** .
If you want to talk about the thing you like less, use **to**.

> He doesn't really like going out. **He prefers** to stay in and read
>   a good book.
> **I prefer** going to the movies **to** watching DVDs at home.
> **I prefer** having dinner at home **to** eating out.

Expressing opinions

Use **I thought ...** to give your opinion of a movie you have seen, a concert you
have been to, or something else that you have done.

> **I thought** it was a really good movie.
> **I thought** the play was a little long.
> **I thought** it was an excellent concert.

If you want to ask other people if they think something is good or bad, use
What did you think of ... ?

> **What did you think of** the band?
> **What did you think of** her voice?
> **What did you think of** the meal?

Useful words

excellent	extremely good
your voice	the sound that comes out from your mouth when you speak or sing

You can also ask someone for their opinion by saying **What's your opinion of ... ?**

> **What's your opinion of** her latest movie?
> **What's your opinion of** the new club that just opened on Kerbey Lane?

To agree with someone's opinion, use **I agree**. If you want to say who you agree with, use **with**.

> "This is a really cool nightclub." "**I agree**."
> **I agree with** Francine. It's a fantastic restaurant.
> I completely **agree with** you. It was a terrible game.

You can also use **You're right ...** to agree with what someone has said.

> "**You're right**. She can't sing!"
> I think **you're right**. His first movie was much better.
> Luca**'s right**. The food here is great.

If you do not agree with someone, you can use **I don't agree.** This is quite strong, so to be very polite, you might say **I'm afraid I don't agree** or **I don't really agree.** You could also use **I disagree ...** . If you want to say who you disagree with, use **with**.

> "It's a great venue." "**I don't really agree**. I think it's too small for this number of people."
> "Anyway, Carla seemed happy enough with her party." "**I don't agree**. I thought she seemed a bit disappointed."
> "It was such a boring movie." "**I don't agree with** you. I thought it was great."

Useful words

cool	fashionable and interesting
a nightclub	a place where people go late in the evening to dance
fantastic	very good
a venue	the place where an event or an activity happens
disappointed	sad because something has not happened or because something is not as good as you hoped

"I think the nightlife in the city has really improved." "I'm afraid **I disagree**." I'm afraid **I disagree with** you there.

I disagree with Martin. There's not much for young people to do in the evening.

You can also use **I don't think ...** to disagree with someone.

"That restaurant has really improved." "**I don't think** it has. I had a really bad meal there a month ago."

"It's the best club in town." "**I don't think** so. I prefer Club 86."

"It was a good show, but it was too long." "Did you think so? **I didn't think** it was."

Asking if something is allowed or permitted

If you need to ask if you can do something when you are out, the simplest way is to use **Can I ... ?**

Can I pay by credit card?
Can we sit outside?

Another way is to use **May I ... ?**

May I take this chair?
May I sit anywhere?

If you want to make sure that someone will not be unhappy or angry if you do something, use **Do you mind if ... ?**

Do you mind if I get to the restaurant a little later?
Do you mind if I join you?
Do you mind if we sit here?

Useful words
nightlife   entertainment at night
join   to come together with other people

You can also use **Is it OK ... ?** This is slightly informal, but you can use it in most situations.

> **Is it OK** to take my cell in with me?
> **Is it OK** to leave my bag here?
> **Is it OK** to eat inside the theater?

To ask if something is allowed, use **Are we allowed to ... ?**

> **Are we allowed to** take pictures?
> **Are we allowed to** ask questions during the lecture?

● Listen for

Here are some important phrases that are connected with going out.

Are you free tomorrow night?
What are you doing tonight?
Would you like to go out?
How about next week?
When would be a good time for you?
I'm afraid I'm busy.
I'm busy next week.
I'd love to.
Maybe another time.

Where would you like to sit?
Smoking or non-smoking?
Can I see your tickets, please?
Would you like to buy a program?

Let me get you a drink.
What can I get you?
Did you have a good time tonight?
Thank you for inviting me.
It was a great party.
We really enjoyed the party.

Useful words
free   not doing anything else and so able to do something
busy   already doing something, so that you are not free to do
                something else

Listen to the conversation: Track 9

Emma and Ashley are talking about Ashley's birthday.

A So what are you doing for your birthday? Have you decided?

B I'm not sure. I might just have a few friends come over in the evening.

A If the weather's nice, you could have a barbecue.

B That's a good idea. I love eating outside when the weather's nice.

A I could help, if you like.

B That would be great — thanks! I'll probably need help because I'm hoping to spend the day with my parents. We're going to meet for lunch.

A That should be nice.

B I think so, but it means I won't have a lot of time to get ready.

A Why don't you ask everyone to bring a dish? That should make things simpler.

B That's a really good idea.

A OK, so what should I bring?

B How about that delicious salad you made for Gina's party?

A Sure. I can make dessert, too. What about a chocolate cake?

B That'd be great! I guess I'd better start inviting people. I'm having dinner with Tina and Jake tonight — I'll ask them then.

 Listen to more phrases and practice saying them: Track 10

Days out

Have a nice day!

If you are planning to see the sights in a city or country, these phrases will help you to ask where you can go, what you can do there, and how much it will cost.

Saying what you want to do

The simplest way of saying what you want to do is to use **I'd like to ...** .

> **I'd like to** go to the aquarium.
> **We'd like to** climb the tower.

If you are very eager to do something, use **I'd really like to ...** or **I'd love to ...** .

> **I'd really like to** see the Great Wall of China.
> **I'd really like to** take some pictures of the town.

> **I'd love to** go hiking in the mountains.
> **I'd love to** visit the palace.

Use **I'd rather ...** when you want to do one thing more than another. If you want to mention the thing that you do not want, use **than**.

> **I'd rather** go to the beach **than** see an art exhibit.
> **We'd rather** take a boat trip **than** go for a walk.
> **I'd rather** visit some of the ancient Roman ruins.

Useful words

an aquarium	a building where fish and sea animals are kept
a tower	a tall, narrow building, or a tall part of another building
a palace	a large, grand building where a king or a queen lives
an exhibit	a public display of art or other objects
ancient	very old, or from a long time ago
ruins	the parts of a building that remain after something destroys the rest

Talking about your plans

We often use **I'm + -ing verb** or **I'm going to ...** to talk about plans for a day out.

> **I'm going** to the Smithsonian tomorrow.
> **We're taking** my parents to the theater.
> **She's seeing** the Monet exhibit this afternoon.

> **I'm going to** check that the museum's open on Mondays.
> **He's going to** hire a guide for the day.
> **We're going to** take the kids with us.

Use **Are you going to ... ?** or **Will you ... ?** to ask someone about their plans.

> **Are you going to** buy a travel guide?
> **Are you going to** visit the Acropolis?

> **Will you** spend all day at the museum?
> **Will you** have time to see the gardens?

You can also use **I'm planning to ...** or **I'm hoping to ...** to say what you intend to do. **I'm hoping to ...** is less definite.

> **I'm planning to** visit Niagara Falls while I'm in Canada.
> **She's planning to** spend the day at the botanic gardens.
> **We're planning to** take a picnic to the beach.

Useful words

hire	to pay someone to do a job for you
a guide	someone who shows tourists around places such as museums or cities
a travel guide	a book for tourists that gives information about a town, an area, or a country
botanic gardens	a place with interesting plants, trees, and grass that people can visit
a picnic	a meal that is eaten outdoors

I'm **hoping to** be able to see the rock paintings.
I'm **hoping to** go on a walk in the rainforest.
We're **hoping to** see some dolphins.

To talk about what should happen in the future, use **I'm supposed to ...** .

I'm **supposed to** bring a picnic lunch.
What time **are we supposed to** get there?
He's **supposed to** meet me this morning.

Making suggestions

The simplest way to make a suggestion is to use **You could ...** .

You could go on a guided tour of the city.
We could ask Jane to show us the old town.

To make a suggestion about something you think would be good to do with other people, use **Should we ... ?**

Should we go to the beach?
Should we try to climb to the top?

Useful words

a rainforest	a thick forest of tall trees that grows in tropical areas
a dolphin	a large gray or black and white intelligent animal that lives in the sea
a guided tour	a trip around an interesting place with someone who tells you about it

Use **How about ... ?** if you have an idea about what to do.

> **How about** taking a boat trip around the harbor?
> **How about** going to the Picasso Museum?

> **GOOD TO KNOW!**
> **How about + -ing**
> The verb that comes after **How about** must be in the -ing form.

Another way to make a suggestion is to say **Why don't ... ?**

> **Why don't** we see if the castle is open to the public?
> **Why don't** we go for a walk in the woods?
> **Why don't** you take her to the street fair?

We should ... is a slightly stronger way of making a suggestion.

> **We should** go to the visitor center first.
> **You should** take a map with you.
> **She should** meets us in the park.

> **GOOD TO KNOW!**
> After **We should**, the verb that follows "I/you/we, etc." is in the simple
> present tense.

> **We should** visit the Met before we leave New York.
> **We should** take some pictures of Chinatown.
> **They should** go to the car museum.

Useful words

a harbor	an area of water next to the land where boats can safely stay
a fair	an event at which people show and sell goods
a visitor center	a building where you can get information about a place

Asking for information

Use **Is ... ?** to ask general questions.

> **Is** the castle interesting?
> **Is** the museum free on Tuesdays?
> **Is** it far to the ice rink?

Use **Is there ... ?** or **Do you have ... ?** to ask whether something exists.

> Excuse me, **is there** a visitor center near here?
> **Is there** anywhere to leave our coats?
> **Are there** any cheaper tickets?

> **Do you have** parking for disabled people?
> **Do you have** any activities for children?
> **Do you have** a restaurant?

To ask about the time, use **What time ... ?**

> **What time** does the park close?
> **What time** is the next guided tour?
> **What time** do we get there?

To ask about the time that something will take, use **How long ... ?**

> **How long** does the tour last?
> **How long** is the boat trip?
> **How long** does it take to get there?

Useful words

an ice rink	a place where people go to skate
a tourist	a person who is visiting a place on vacation
disabled	having a physical or mental condition that makes it difficult for you to do some things

To ask how to do something, use **How do you ... ?**

> **How do you** get to the old part of town?
> **How do you** reserve tickets?
> **How do you** reserve a table?

> **GOOD TO KNOW!**
> **How do you + infinitive**
> The verb that comes after **How do you** must be in the base form.

Asking for things

To ask for something, use **Can I have ... ?**, **Could I have ... ?**, or **I'd like ...** .
To be very polite, use **please**.

> **Can I have** two tickets for tonight's performance, please?
> **Can I have** an audio guide, please?

> **Could I have** a program for this evening's concert?
> **Could we have** three seats together?

> **I'd like** a map of the area, please.
> **I'd like** front row seats, if possible.

Useful words

reserve	to ask a hotel or a restaurant to keep a room or a table for you
a performance	when you entertain an audience by singing, dancing, or acting
an audio guide	a piece of equipment that gives you spoken information about a place
a program	a small book or piece of paper that tells you about a play or concert
front row	in the line of seats at the front of a theater

If it is important for you to have something, you can use **I need ...** .

> **I need** the address of the museum.
> **I need** a street map of the city.
> **We need** a guide who speaks English.

If you want to ask if something you want is available, use **Do you have ... ?**

> **Do you have** any brochures in English?
> **Do you have** any information on day trips in this area?
> **Do you have** any tickets for tomorrow's show?

If you are asking someone if they can do something for you, the simplest way is to use **Can you ... ?** or **Could you ... ? Could you ... ?** is slightly more formal than **Can you ... ?**

> **Can you** tell me what the hours are?
> Please **can you** show me where we are on this map?

> **Could you** check if I've got the right tickets?
> **Could you** tell me the way to the theater?

Useful words

a brochure	a thin magazine with pictures that gives you information about a place, a product, or a service
hours	the times that a place opens and closes

A polite way of asking someone to do something is by saying **Would you mind ... ?**

> **Would you mind** showing me where the modern art exhibit is?
> **Would you mind** checking that I've got the right tickets?
> **Would you mind** translating this into English?

To ask whether something you want is possible, use **Is it possible ... ?**

> **Is it possible** to change these tickets for tomorrow's performance?
> **Is it possible** to get cheaper tickets?
> **Is it possible** to hire a Portuguese-speaking guide?

Asking if something is allowed or permitted

If you need to ask if you can do something, the simplest way is to use
Can I ... ?

> **Can I** use this ticket?
> **Can we** park here?

Another way of asking for permission is to use **May I ... ?**

> **May I** borrow this travel guide?
> **May we** look around the gardens?
> **May we** see the room where he worked?

If you want to check that someone will not be unhappy or angry if you do
something, use **Do you mind if ... ?**

> **Do you mind if** we show up a little late?
> **Do you mind if** he brings a friend?
> **Do you mind if** I leave the stroller here?

Useful words

an exhibit	public display of art or other objects
translate	to say or write something again in a different language
show up	to arrive
a stroller	a small chair on wheels used for moving a young child around

You can also use **Is it OK ... ?** This is informal, but you can use it in most situations.

> **Is it OK** to take pictures?
> **Is it OK** to use this entrance?
> **Is it OK** if I record your talk?

To ask if something is allowed, use **Are we allowed to ... ?**

> **Are we allowed to** take drinks inside?
> **Are we allowed to** come back in again later?
> **Are we allowed to** wait here?

Saying what you like, dislike, prefer

The simplest way to talk about things you like is to use **I like ...** . To talk about activities that you like doing, use **I enjoy ...** .

> **I like** visiting modern art galleries.
> **I like** this sculpture very much.
> **Do you like** going to concerts?

> **I enjoy** taking guided tours.
> I really **enjoy** learning about history.
> **Do you enjoy** the ballet?

Useful words	
the entrance	the door or gate where you go into a place
record	to store sounds so that they can be heard again
a gallery	a place where people go to look at art
a sculpture	a piece of art that is made into a shape from a material like stone or wood
ballet	a type of dancing that needs a lot of skill and in which there are many carefully planned movements

> **GOOD TO KNOW!**
> **Like/Enjoy + -ing**
> When **like** or **enjoy** is followed by a verb, the verb is usually in the -ing form.

If you like something very much, you can say **I love ...** .

> **I love** the ruins in Taos.
> **I love** this type of architecture.
> **I love** going to art galleries.

To tell someone what you do not like, use **I don't like ...** , or to make your view stronger, **I hate ...** .

> **I don't like** bus tours.
> **I don't like** roller coasters.
> **I don't like** Shakespeare.

> **I hate** being late.
> I really **hate** horror movies.
> **I hate** taking the subway.

A slightly formal way of saying what you don't like is **I dislike ...** .

> **I dislike** standing in line.
> **She dislikes** taking public transportation.

> **GOOD TO KNOW!**
> **Hate/Dislike + -ing**
> When **hate** or **dislike** is followed by a verb, the verb is usually in the -ing form.

Useful words

architecture	the style of the design of a building
a roller coaster	a thing like a fast train that goes up and down very steep slopes at an amusement park
a horror movie	a very frightening movie that you watch for entertainment.
stand in line	to stand one behind the other in a line of people, waiting for something
public transportion	a system of vehicles such as buses and trains that the public uses

If you want to say that you like one thing more than another, use **I prefer ...** .
If you want to talk about the thing you like less, use **to**.

> **I prefer** science museums **to** art museums.
> **She prefers** walking **to** biking.
> **I prefer** to avoid that area.

To say that you would prefer to do something, use **I'd rather ...** . If you want to talk about the thing you like less, use **than**.

> **I'd rather** do something outdoors **than** go to a museum.
> **I'd rather** spend the whole week in Washington.
> **We'd rather** walk **than** take the bus.

To talk about something that you would prefer not to do, use **I'd prefer not to ...** or **I'd rather not ...** .

> **I'd prefer not to** travel by boat.
> **We'd prefer not to** carry our own luggage.

> **I'd rather not** stay much longer.
> **I'd rather not** go on the roller coaster.

> **GOOD TO KNOW!**
> Remember **that I'd rather not ...** is followed by the base form of
> the verb.

Useful words

avoid	to keep away from a person, place, or thing
outdoors	outside rather than in a building

Complaining

You may have to complain about something you're unhappy with. You could start your complaint with **I'm not happy ...** or **I'm disappointed ...** .

> **I'm not happy** with our guide.
> **I'm not happy** about having to pay extra for the children.
> **I wasn't happy** that the pool was closed.

> **I'm disappointed** with the way we were treated.
> **She was disappointed** about not seeing any lions.
> The children **were disappointed** that they didn't get to see the clowns.

You can use **I think ...** to give your opinion about what is wrong with a place or an event.

> **I think** it's a little expensive for what it is.
> **I think** that they need to clean the rooms more often.
> **I don't think** it's very well organized.
> **I didn't think** the museum was very interesting.
> **I thought** the speakers were badly prepared.

Useful words
a clown   a performer who wears funny clothes and does silly things to
                 make people laugh

● Listen for

Here are some useful phrases you may hear on your day out.

Press here to select the language you want.
Here's a flyer in English.
Do you have a student ID?
The museum's open from nine to three.
The gallery's closed on Sundays.
The next guided tour's at ten.
It's eight dollars a piece.
You're not allowed to take pictures.
Can I search your bag?
Please leave your things in the coatroom.
Please make a donation to support our museum.
Please supervise your children at all times.

Useful words

select	to choose one particular person or thing from a group of similar people or things
a flyer	a piece of paper containing information about a particular subject
a coatroom	a room in a building where you can leave your coat
a donation	money that is given to help an organization
supervise	to make sure that someone behaves well or does something correctly

Listen to the conversation: Track 11

Brett and Emma have decided to spend Saturday together. They're talking about what to do.

A What should we do on Saturday, Emma? I was hoping to see the Monet exhibit some time — would you be interested in doing that?

B The weather's so nice at this time of year, I'd rather do something outside, if you don't mind. How about going to the park?

A That'd be great. What do you want to do about lunch? Is there a café there?

B There is, but it's not very good. We could buy some sandwiches on the way and take them with us.

A Good idea. I'm planning to meet Mario at six, so we'll have to be back by five at the latest.

B That's fine.

Brett has arrived at the Museum of Archaeology and is talking to a member of the staff.

A I'm hoping to see the Roman exhibit. Do you have any information about it?

B We have this brochure.

A How much is it?

B It's five dollars.

A I'll have one, please.

B OK, that's five dollars. Would you like to leave your bag in the coatroom?

A I'd prefer not to — I've got some expensive camera equipment in it. By the way, is it OK to take pictures inside the museum?

B No, I'm sorry, we don't allow cameras.

A That's too bad. I'm supposed to give a talk to my history club, and I wanted to show some pictures.

 Listen to more phrases and practice saying them: Track 12

Shopping

Can I help you?

Whether you're planning to shop for clothes or things for your home, buy food, or just pick up a postcard, this unit will give you all the phrases you need when you go shopping.

Asking for things

The simplest way to ask for something in a store is to use **I'd like ...** or **Could I have ... ?**

>**I'd like** two pounds of potatoes, please.
>**I'd like** a case for my phone.
>**I'd like** a melon that's nice and ripe, please.

>**Could I have** a box of envelopes, please?
>**Could I have** a five-gallon can of white paint?
>**Could I have** a shopping bag, please?

You can also say what you are looking for by using **I'm looking for ...** .

>**I'm looking for** vegetable seeds.
>**I'm looking for** brown rice.

Useful words	
a melon	a large fruit with soft, sweet flesh and hard green or yellow skin
ripe	used for describing fruit or vegetables that are ready to eat
an envelope	the paper cover in which you put a letter before you send it to someone
a shopping bag	a plastic or paper bag for carrying things

To ask if a store sells the thing you want, use **Do you sell ... ?** or **Do you have ... ?**

> **Do you sell** light bulbs?
> **Do you sell** printer paper?
> **Do you sell** plant pots?

> **Do you have** any white shirts?
> **Do you have** a battery that will fit my hearing aid?
> **Do you have** the shoelaces for these shoes?

In a shop where an assistant fetches things, you could say **Can you give me ... , please?**

> **Can you give me** five oranges, **please?**
> **Can you give me** ten first-class stamps, **please?**
> **Can you give me** three yards of this cloth, **please?**

When you have decided what you want to buy, use **I'll have ...** or **I'd like ...** .

> **I'll take** the handbag.
> **I'll take** the big saucepan.
> **I'll take** two of those pineapples.

> **I'd like** some bananas.
> **I'd like** a loaf of wholewheat bread.
> **I'd like** three dozen red roses.

Useful words

a hearing aid	a small piece of equipment that people wear in their ear to help them to hear better
shoelaces	the cords used to fasten shoes
wholegrain	made using whole seeds
a dozen	twelve

Saying what you have to do

If you need to buy something, use **I have to ...** or **I've got to ...** .

I have to buy Richard a birthday card.
I have to stop at the bakery.
You have to ask the salesperson if you want to try things on.
We have to buy a new vacuum cleaner.

I've got to get a memory stick.
I've got to order the books in time for school.
I've got to buy some food for tonight.

You could also use **I need to ...** .

I need to get something to wear to Joe and Flora's wedding.
I need to make sure I get receipts for everything.
I need to take back that MP3 player I bought.

Useful words

a vacuum cleaner	an electric machine that cleans surfaces by sucking up dust and dirt
a memory stick	a small electronic device for storing computer information
order	to ask for something to be sent to you from a company
a receipt	a piece of paper that shows that you have paid for something

Use **I should ...** to talk about things you feel you ought to do.

> **I should** buy some low-energy light bulbs.
> **I should** shop locally more often.
> **I should** try the mechanic Frank recommended.

Talking about your plans

To tell someone what you are going to do, use **I'm going to ...** or **I'll ...** .

> **I'm going to** buy new carpet.
> **I'm going to** wait for it to go on sale.
> **We're going to** go to the mall.
> **Are you going to** get a bigger TV?

> **I'll** get some flowers for Diana.
> **I'll** try to find a duvet cover that matches the curtains.
> **I'll** find out how much a new printer would cost.

To tell someone about a plan you have, use **I'm planning to ...** .

> **I'm planning to** buy a new outfit for the party.
> **I'm planning to** buy him a tennis racket for his birthday.
> **I'm planning to** spend the day shopping.

Useful words

locally	in the area where you live
recommend	to suggest that someone would find a particular person or thing good or useful
the sales	a time when a shop sells things for less that their normal price
a duvet	a thick warm cover for a bed
match	to have the same colour or design as another thing, or to look good with it
an outfit	a set of clothes

You may want to talk about what you're thinking of buying or where you're thinking of going. Use **I'm thinking of...** .

> **I'm thinking of** going to the mall tomorrow.
> **I'm thinking of** getting a laptop.
> **We're thinking of** buying a boat.

For something you would like to do, but that is not certain, use **I'm hoping to ...** .

> **I'm hoping to** find some bargains.
> **I'm hoping to** find some boots.
> **We're hoping to** visit some antique shops.

Expressing opinions

When you look at things in a store, you may want to say what you think of them. Use **I think ...** .

> **I think** this material is beautiful.
> **I think** their cakes are the best in town.
> **I don't think** she'd like that bracelet.

You can also use **In my opinion ...** .

> **In my opinion** the quality of their products has gone down.
> **In my opinion** this lipstick is slightly too dark.
> Where's the best place to buy a bike, **in your opinion**?

Useful words

an antique	an old object that is valuable because of its beauty or because of the way it was made
a bracelet	a piece of jewelry that you wear around your wrist
lipstick	a colored substance that women sometimes put on their lips

Another way to give your opinion is to use **I'd say ...** .

> **I'd say** it's a little tight.
> **I'd say** that you need something warmer for winter.
> **I'd say** it's a bargain.

To agree with someone's else's opinion, use **I agree** or **You're right.**

> "The assistants here are fantastic." "**I agree**. They're always happy to give advice."
> **I agree** with Helen that the leather chairs are more practical.
> "The lighter jacket is more suitable for summer." "**I agree.**"

> "It's too tight around the waist." "**You're right.** I need a bigger size."
> **You're right** about this place — it's improved a lot since the new manager took over.
> "It's not worth buying cheap clothes — they won't last." "**You're right.** It's better to spend more and buy less."

To disagree, you can say **I don't think so**. You can also say **I disagree** but this is quite strong.

> "These linen trousers would be good for the journey." "**I don't think so** — they crease too easily."
> "Alla would love this shirt." "**I don't** really **think so** — she prefers bright colours."
> "The assistants were so rude." "**I didn't think so** — that young man was very helpful."

Useful words

tight	small, and fitting closely to your body
leather	animal skin that is used for making shoes, clothes, bags and furniture
practical	useful rather than being just fashionable or attractive
suitable	right for a particular purpose or occasion
your waist	the middle part of your body
take something over	to get control of something
linen	a type of strong cloth
crease	to form lines when pressed or folded
helpful	helping you by being useful or willing to work for you

"Buying organic food is a waste of money." "**I disagree**. It's good for you and good for the environment."

I disagree with what Naeem said about the butcher's.

"It's cheaper to buy larger quantities of food." "**I disagree** – if you do that, you end up throwing away a lot of it."

If you are shopping with someone else, you may want to ask for that person's opinion about something you are thinking of buying. Use **What do you think ... ?**

What do you think of these jeans?

What do you think of their furniture?

What do you think about buying a picnic blanket?

Asking for information

For general information, use **Could you tell me ... ?**

Could you tell me if there's a book store here?

Could you tell me where I can get weedkiller?

Could you tell me the best place for children's clothes?

If you want to ask if a town has a particular shop, use **Is there ... ?**

Is there anywhere I can recharge my phone?

Is there a florist in this town?

Is there a butcher's?

Useful words

organic	grown without using chemicals
a butcher's	a shop where you can buy meat
weedkiller	a substance that kills weeds (= plants that you do not want)
a florist	a shop where you can buy flowers

For asking where a shop is, or where something is in a store, use **Where can I find ... ?**

> **Where can I find** a hardware store?
> **Where can I find** underwear?
> **Where can I find** the new Jacqueline Wilson book?

You can use **Is there ... ?** or **Do you have ... ?** to ask if a store has something.

> **Is there** a dressing room?
> **Is there** anyone who can explain the difference between these washing machines?
> **Is there** a garden department?

> **Do you have** any dinner plates?
> **Do you have** it in a smaller size?
> **Do you have** any sunhats?

To ask for information about something you might buy, use **Is this ... ?** or **Is it ... ?**

> **Is this** the best model?
> **Is this** available in any different colors?
> **Are these** on sale?

> **Is it** genuine leather?
> **Is it** suitable for a child?
> **Are they** still in stock?

Useful words

hardware	tools and equipment that are used in the home and garden
underwear	clothes that you wear next to your skin, under your other clothes
a dressing room	a room in a clothes shop where you can try on clothes
a model	a particular design of something
genuine	true and real
in stock	available for you to buy

To ask a sales person for advice about what to buy, use **What would you recommend ... ?**

> **What would you recommend** for painting iron railings?
> I'm looking for some garden furniture that will be OK in the rain.
>   **What would you recommend?**
> **What would you recommend** for dry hair?

To ask for the price of something, use **How much is ... ?**

> **How much is** the face cream?
> **How much are** the cherries per kilo?
> **How much are** your pineapples?

To ask whether you can do something, use **Can I ... ?**

> **Can I** pay by credit card?
> **Can I** have it giftwrapped?
> **Can you** give me a discount, as it has a scratch on it?

Saying what you like, dislike, prefer

The simplest way to say what you like when you are shopping is **I like ...** .

> **I like** Italian cheese.
> **I like** this hat very much.
> Get it if **you like** it.
> **I don't like** the pattern.
> **I don't like** these gloves as much.

Useful words

a railing	a fence that is made from metal bars
per	for each
giftwrap	to put colored paper around something so that it can be given as a present
a discount	a reduction in the usual price of something
a pattern	an arrangement of lines or shapes that form a design
a glove	a piece of clothing that you wear on your hand, with a separate part for each finger

If you have strong feelings about something, you could use **I love ...** or **I hate ...** .

> **I love** these chocolates.
> **I love** shopping with friends.
> **I love** trying on expensive clothes.

> **I hate** standing in line.
> **I hate** dresses like this.
> **I hate** egg plants.

> **GOOD TO KNOW!**
> **Like/Love/Hate + -ing**
> When **like**, **love**, or **hate** are followed by a verb, the verb is usually in the -ing form.

To say that you like one thing more than another, use **I prefer ...** . If you want to talk about the thing you like less, use **to**.

> **I prefer** the one with the long sleeves.
> **We prefer** fresh produce **to** frozen.
> **I prefer** to buy things from independent stores.

To say what you would prefer to do, use **I'd rather ...** . If you want to talk about the thing you do not want to do, use **than** before it.

> **I'd rather** go for something more glamorous.
> **I'd rather** spend the money on CDs **than** books.
> **We'd rather** buy local produce.

Useful words	
an egg plant	a vegetable with a smooth, dark purple skin
a sleeve	one of the two parts of a piece of clothing that cover your arms
independent	not owned by a large company
glamorous	very attractive, exciting or interesting
local	in, or relating to, the area where you live
produce	food that you grow on a farm to sell

Making suggestions

If you are shopping with a friend, use **We could ...** to make suggestions.

> **We could** ask them to deliver it.
> **We could** see if they'll order one for us.
> **You could** ask them for a discount.

If you have an idea about something, use **How about ... ?**

> **How about** going shopping this morning?
> **How about** trying that new bookshop?
> **How about** buying it online?

> **GOOD TO KNOW!**
> **How about + -ing**
> The verb that comes after **How about** must be in the -ing form.

You could also use **Why don't ... ?** or **Why not ... ?**

> **Why don't** you wait for the sales?
> **Why don't** you treat yourself to a new suit?
> **Why don't** we look in another store?

> **Why not** buy both shirts?
> **Why not** try it on?
> **Why not** ask David to pay for it?

> **GOOD TO KNOW!**
> **Why not + infinitive**
> The verb that comes after **Why not** must be in the infinitive without "to."

Useful words
deliver   to take something to a particular place

Asking for permission

To ask someone in a shop if you can do something, use **Can I ... ?**

> **Can I** try on these sandals?
> **Can I** keep the hanger?
> **Can I** bring it back if I don't like it?
> **Can I** use this coupon to pay for it?
> **Can my daughter** try on this jacket?

A polite way of asking for permission is **Do you mind if I ... ?**

> **Do you mind if I** try the other pants on again?
> **Do you mind if I** take the wrapper off?
> **Do you mind if I** pay by credit card?

A slightly informal way of asking for permission is **Is it OK ... ?**

> **Is it OK** if I have a closer look?
> **Is it OK** if I taste one of these cherries?
> **Is it OK** if I take the watch out of its box?

Useful words

a sandal	a light shoe that you wear in warm weather
a hanger	an object for hanging clothes on
a coupon	a piece of paper that can be used instead of money to pay for things
a wrapper	a piece of paper or plastic that covers something you buy

● Listen for

Here are some useful phrases you may hear when out shopping.

Are you being served?
Can I help you?
How much were you thinking of spending?
We don't have any in stock just now.
We could order one for you, if you like.
We may have one in our other store.
Is there anything else?
Is it a gift?
Would you like me to giftwrap it for you?
Would you like to keep the hanger?
Cash only, I'm afraid.
I'm afraid we don't take credit cards.
Could you sign here, please?
That comes to $34.57.
Please enter your PIN.
You can take your card now.
We don't give refunds on sale items.
Do you have your receipt?

Useful words
a refund   an amount of money that is returned to you because you have
                    returned goods to a store

Listen to the conversation: Track 13

Brett has invited some friends for dinner. He goes to the Italian deli to buy food and to get some advice about what to cook.

A Hi. I'm making dinner for five people tomorrow evening. I need to get something that'll be quick so that I have time to prepare it after work.

B How about pasta? That's always popular, and we sell delicious fresh pasta.

A That sounds great. Can you give me enough for five people, please? And what would you recommend for the sauce?

B Why not try something spicy — maybe tomato with chilli, garlic, and spicy sausage?

A I don't think my friend Ella would like that — she doesn't eat meat.

B You could use olives instead of the sausage. We have a great selection of olives.

A Hmm. Could I taste one of these?

B Sure.

A These are great. I'll take a large jar of the black ones. I'm also looking for something for dessert.

B We have delicious biscotti, made with sugar, dried fruit, and nuts. They're great with coffee. Or we have lots of great cakes, if you prefer.

A I was planning to make a cake myself, but I would like some biscotti. Can I pay by credit card?

Useful words
a deli   a store that sells food such as cold meat and cheeses

B Of course. Anything else?

A No, I think that's everything. Thanks for your help.

 Listen to more phrases and practice saying them: Track 14

Service with a smile

Excellent service!

If you need a service of some sort, or need help or information, these phrases will help you say what you want and ask for what you need.

Greetings

Use **Hello** as a general greeting to people in store, banks, etc. It is polite to say **Hello** to anyone in any situation.

> **Hello**, ma'am.
> **Hello**. I wonder if you can help me.

Use **Hi** to greet people in more informal situations, for example a café or a salon.

> **Hi**, I have an appointment with Freya for a haircut at 10:00.
> **Hi**, I'd like to make an appointment with Morgan.

You can use **Good morning, Good afternoon,** or **Good evening** in slightly more formal situations.

> **Good morning**. I'd like some information about travel insurance.

Use **Goodbye** when you leave a store, bank, etc.

> Thanks for all your help. **Goodbye**.

Useful words

a salon	a place where you go to have your hair cut, or to have a beauty treatment
an appointment	an arrangement to see someone at a particular time
insurance	an agreement that you make with a company in which you pay money to them regularly, and they pay you if something bad happens to you or your property

Goodbye is often shortened to **Bye**. **Bye** is slightly informal.

> Thanks very much. **Bye**.

See you is an informal way of saying goodbye, for example to a hairdresser that you know you will see again.

> Thanks very much. **See you** soon!
> Thanks, Louisa. **See you** in a couple of months.

People often say **Have a good day!** or **Have a good weekend!** as you are leaving.

> Goodbye, **have a good day!**
> Bye, **have a good weekend!**

Talking about yourself

Often you will need to tell people information about yourself, such as your name and where you live. To say what your name is, use **My name is ...** .

> **My name is** Ray Weaver.
> **My wife's name is** Emilia Gomez.

To say where you live, use **my address is ...** .

> **My address is** 29 Knoll Road, Austin, TX 78759.
> **My address** in New Zealand **is** 6 Green Street, Wellington.
> **My** permanent **address is** 257 West 84 Street, New York, NY, 10024.

Useful words
a couple	two or around two people or things
permanent	continuing forever or for a very long time

To say which country you were born in and lived in as a child, use **I'm from ...** .

> **I'm from** Algeria.
> **I'm from** Buenos Aires, Argentina.
> **We're from** South Korea.

If you want to say that you are living somewhere for a short time, for example because you are on vacation, use **I'm staying ...** .

> **I'm staying** with a host family.
> **We're staying** in a rented house.

Saying what you have to do

To say what service or help you need, you can use **I have to ...** or **I need to ...** .

> **I have to** find out when they're going to deliver my television.
> **I have to** pick up my jacket from the dry cleaner's.

> **I need to** get my hair cut.
> **I need to** see a dentist.

To ask what someone has to do, use **Do you have to ... ?**

> **Do you have to** speak to someone at the bank?
> **Do you have to** show your passport?

Useful words

a host	someone who invites people to stay in their home
rented	used by people who pay money to the owner
find out	to learn the facts about something
deliver	to take something to a particular place
a dry cleaner's	a store where clothes are cleaned with a special chemical rather than water
a dentist	a person whose job is to examine and treat people's teeth

When you want to say that you should do something, use **I should ...** .

> **I should** drop by the real estate agent's office on my way home.
> **You should** reschedule the appointment.
> I suppose **I should** call them to cancel the appointment.
> **You shouldn't** throw it away before you've tried to fix it.

> **GOOD TO KNOW!**
> **Should + infinitive**
> The verb that comes after **should** is in the base form.

To say what you cannot do, use **I cannot/can't ...** .

> **I can't** be late for my appointment.
> **I can't** forget that my suit is at the dry-cleaner's.
> **You can't** miss your appointment this time.

Useful words

a real estate agent	a person whose job is to sell buildings or land
reschedule	to arrange for an event to happen at a different time
cancel	to say that something that has been planned will not happen
throw something away	to get rid of something that you do not want

Saying what you want to do

The simplest way to say what you would like to do is to use **I'd like to ...** .

> **I'd like to** find out about the various kinds of accounts that are available.
> **I'd like to** transfer some money.
> **I'd like to** get this jacket dry cleaned.

If you are very eager to do something, use **I'd really like to ...** or **I'd love to ...** .

> **I'd really like to** change my bank account.
> **I'd really like to** find out about other services.
> **I'd really like to** speak to someone who can help me.

> **I'd love to** get my hair cut.
> **I'd love to** get some new glasses.

An informal way of saying that you would like to do or have something is
I wouldn't mind ... .

> **I wouldn't mind** going to the bank on the way there.
> **I wouldn't mind** stopping off at the bank.

> **GOOD TO KNOW!**
> **I wouldn't mind + -ing**
> The verb that comes after **I wouldn't mind** must be in the -ing form.

Useful words

various	of several different types
an account	an arrangement with a bank where they look after your money for you
transfer	to make something or someone go from one place to another
dry clean	to clean clothes with a special chemical rather than water
stop off	to visit somewhere for a short time on your way to somewhere else

Asking for information

Use **Is ... ?** to ask general questions requiring information.

> **Is** the bank far from here?
> **Is** it far to the post office?

Use **Is there ... ?** or **Do you have ... ?** to ask whether something exists.

> Excuse me, **is there** a pharmacy near here?
> **Is there** an Internet café in the area?

> **Do you have** any other types of accounts?
> **Do you have** an account manager that I can talk to?

To ask about the time that something will happen, use **What time ... ?** or **When ... ?**

> **What time** does the bank close?
> **What time** do I need to be here?

> **When** is the appointment?
> **When** should I come back?

To ask about the price of something, use **How much ... ?**

> **How much** is the service?
> **How much** is an eye exam?
> **How much** would you charge to fix these shoes?

Useful words

a pharmacy	a place where you can buy medicines
an Internet cafe	a café where there are computers which allow you to use the Internet
an account manager	an expert whose job is to help bank customers

To ask how much time something will take, use **How long ... ?**

> **How long** is the appointment?
> **How long** do I have to wait to see someone?

To ask how to do something, use **How do you ... ?**

> **How do you** open a bank account?
> **How do you** send money to the UK?

> **GOOD TO KNOW!**
> **How do you + infinitive**
> The verb that comes after **How do you** must be in the base form.

Asking for things

To ask for something, use **Can I have ... ?**, **Could I have ... ?**, or **I'd like ...** .
To be very polite, use **please**.

> **Can I have** a receipt, please?
> **Can I have** a photocopy of the document, please?
> Please **can I have** a brochure?

> **Could I have** a flyer, please?
> **Could I have** some information, please?
> **Could I have** a list of prices, please?

Useful words

a bank account	an arrangement with a bank where they look after your money for you
a receipt	a piece of paper that shows you have received goods or money from someone
a photocopy	a copy of a document that you make using a special machine
a document	an official piece of paper with important information on it
a brochure	a thin magazine with pictures that gives you information about a product or a service
a flyer	a piece of paper containing information about a particular subject

I'd like some help, please.
I'd like an appointment next week, please.
I'd like your opinion.

If it is important for you to have something, you can use **I need ...** .

I need some help.
I need to get the money there quickly.
We need your signature.
You need some form of identification.

If you want to ask if something you want is available, use **Do you have ... ?**

Do you have your passport with you?
Do you have a fax machine?
Do you have your documents with you?

If you are asking someone if they can do something for you, the simplest way is to use **Can you ... ?** or **Could you ... ? Could you ... ?** is slightly more formal than **Can you ... ?**

Can you call me when it's ready to be picked up, please?
Can you tell me how much it will be?

Could you fax it to me, please?
Could you take a look at my camera, please?

Useful words

a signature	your name written in your own special way
a fax machine	a special machine that is joined to a telephone line and that you use to send and receive documents
to fax	to send a document to another fax machine

Another way of asking someone to do something is by saying **Would you mind ... ?**

> **Would you mind** giving me a photocopy of the contract?
> **Would you mind** giving me an estimate?
> **Would you mind** emailing me the details, please?

To ask whether something you want is possible, use **Is it possible ... ?**

> **Is it possible** to get an earlier appointment?
> **Is it possible** to speak to the manager?
> **Is it possible** to pay in installments?

Making suggestions

The simplest way to make a suggestion about what to do or buy is to use **You could ...** .

> **You could** come back tomorrow.
> **You could** find out the details online.
> Instead of buying a new one, **you could** repair your old one.

If two or more people are trying to decide what to do or buy, use **Should we ... ?**

> **Should we** try a different hairdresser?
> **Should we** come back later and see if they're open?
> **Should we** ask for a refund?

Useful words

a contract	an official agreement between two companies or people
an estimate	a guess of how much you think something will cost
an installment	one of several small regular payments that you make over a period of time
a refund	money that is returned to you because you have paid too much, or because you have returned goods to a store

Use **How about ... ?** if you have an idea about what to do or buy.

> **How about** changing the appointment to Friday?
> **How about** asking to speak to the manager?
> **How about** changing your bank?

> **GOOD TO KNOW!**
> **How about + -ing**
> The verb that comes after **How about** must be in the -ing form.

Another way to make a suggestion is to say **Why don't ... ?**

> **Why don't** you use the laundromat on Elm Street?
> **Why don't** you get the TV fixed?
> **Why don't** you exchange the bike for a bigger one?

I suggest ... and **You should ...** are slightly stronger ways of making a suggestion.

> **I suggest** you contact your bank in the US.
> **I suggest** you find a new cleaning service.
> **I suggest** you get the locks on your doors replaced.

> **GOOD TO KNOW!**
> After **I suggest**, the verb that follows must be in the base form.

Useful words

a laundromat	a place where people pay to use machines to wash and dry their clothes
exchange	to take something back to a shop and get a different thing
contact	to telephone someone or send them a message or a letter
a lock	a device which prevents something from being opened except with a particular key
replace	to get something new in the place of something that is damaged or lost

We should try to agree a price first.
We should open a savings account.
They should complain about the poor service.

Talking about your plans

Use **I'm + -ing verb** or **I'm going to ...** to talk about plans that you are sure of.

> **I'm having** a new key made this morning.
> **She's meeting** a financial adviser this afternoon to talk about her pension.

> **I'm going to** change my hairdresser.
> **I'm going to** complain about the service that we received.

To talk about your plans, you can also use **I'm planning to ...** or, if you are slightly less sure, **I'm hoping to ...** .

> **I'm planning to** rent a car for the weekend.
> **I'm planning to** use caterers for the party.

> **I'm hoping to** get to the bank today.
> **She's hoping to** get the bike fixed.

Useful words

savings	all the money that you have saved, especially in a bank
poor	bad
a key	a specially shaped piece of metal that opens or closes a lock
financial	relating to money
a pension	money that you regularly receive after you retire
rent	to pay to use something for a short time
a caterer	a company that provides food and drink at a party

To talk about a plan that is only possible, use **I might ...** .

> **I might** have the party professionally catered.
> **I might** ask Kelly to help me.

To talk about something that should happen in the future, use **I'm supposed to ...** .

> **I'm supposed to** provide original documents.
> What time **are we supposed to** be there?
> **He's supposed to** pay the band.

Useful words

professionally	by someone who does something as a job rather than for enjoyment
original	not copied, but being the first

● Listen for

Here are some phrases you are likely to hear in banks, hairdressers and other places that provide services.

Can I help you?
Can I help you at all?
Can I get you anything else?
Could I ask a few questions, please?
It'll be ready tomorrow.
It's not ready yet.
Do you have your receipt?
Do you need a receipt?
Remember to keep your receipts.
Do you have some form of identification?
Do you have your passport?
I'll need to see some form of identification.
When would you like to come in?
Do you have an appointment?
Please call back tomorrow.
How would you like to pay?
Do you need a deposit?
I'll pay the full amount later.

Useful words
a deposit   a sum of money that is part of the full price of something, and that you pay when you agree to buy it

Listen to the conversation: Track 15

Ashley is talking to a real estate agent. She's looking for a new apartment.

A Hello, can I help you?

B Yes, I'm looking for an apartment to rent downtown.

A Certainly. I just need to ask a few questions first.

B Sure.

A OK, what's your name?

B It's Ashley Brooks.

A And where do you live?

B 1505 Parker Street, Englewood.

A And you'd like to live downtown?

B That's right.

A What exactly are you looking for?

B I'd really like a three bedroom.

A And when would you like to move in?

B I'm hoping to be there by September — I'm starting a new job in October.

A OK, let's see. How about this one? It has three bedrooms and it's near Larimer Square.

B It's very nice, but it's kind of expensive. Do you have anything a little cheaper?

A What about this one? It's cheaper and just a little smaller — and it still has three bedrooms.

B That sounds good. Do you have any information I can take home to show my friend?

A Of course. Why don't you take this flyer with you and get back to me when you've made a decision?

B Thanks, I will.

 Listen to more phrases and practice saying them: Track 16

Health

Get well soon!

If you get sick, have an accident, or need other medical attention, the phrases in this chapter will allow you to talk to a doctor, dentist, or pharmacist. Use them to get the advice or treatment that you need.

Describing the problem

If you need to describe a medical problem, you can use **I have ...** .

> **I have** a temperature.
> **I have** a rash.
> **I have** high blood pressure.

If you want to say which part of your body hurts, use **My ... hurts**. If the pain you have is an ache, you can say which part of your body it is in by using **I have a/an ... ache**.

> **My** back **hurts**.
> **His** foot **hurts**.
> **It hurts** here.

> **I have** a head**ache**.
> **I have** a stomach**ache**.
> **She has** a tooth**ache**.

You can talk about more general problems using **I feel ...** .

> **I feel** tired all the time.
> **I feel** like I'm getting a cold.

Useful words

your temperature	how hot someone's body is
a rash	an area of red spots on your skin
your blood pressure	the pressure at which blood flows around your body

I've been feeling dizzy.
I've been feeling depressed.

If you want to tell a doctor about a problem you have, use **I'm ...** .

I'm allergic to penicillin.
I'm diabetic.
I'm on heart medication.

Saying what happened

If you have an accident, you will need to explain what happened. You will need to use a past tense, such as **I fell ...** or **I burned ...** .

I bumped my head on a shelf.
I fell down the stairs.
She burned herself on the stove.
I tripped on the curb.

If your medical problem means that you cannot do something that you should be able to do, you can use **I can't ...** .

I can't put any weight on that foot.
I can't straighten my arm.
She can't bend her arm.

Useful words

dizzy	having the feeling that you are about to fall
depressed	feeling very sad for a long time
allergic	becoming ill when you eat, touch, or breathe something
penicillin	a type of medicine that kills bacteria
diabetic	having an illness where you cannot control the level of sugar in your blood
medication	medicine that is used for treating an illness
trip	to knock your foot against something and fall
a curb	the edge of a pavement
straighten	to make something straight

If you hurt a part of your body as the result of an accident, you can use phrases such as **I broke ...** or **I sprained ...** to describe your injury.

> I think **I broke** my arm.
> **She broke** her toe.
> **I sprained** my wrist.
> **I twisted** my ankle.

Asking for information

When you need to get information about someone or something, you can use simple questions starting with **What ... ?**, **Which ... ?**, **How ... ?**, **Who ... ?**, or **When ... ?**

> **What** do I ask the pharmacist for?
> **Which** floor is she on?
> **How** do I make an appointment?
> **Who** did you see last time?
> **When** does visiting time start?

To ask where something is, use **Where can I find ... ?** For more general information, you could say **Could you tell me ... ?** or **I'd like to know ...** . If you need to get someone's attention to ask a question, first say **Excuse me**.

> Excuse me, **where can I find** a pharmacy?
> Excuse me, **where can I find** a dentist?
> Excuse me, **where can I find** a wheelchair?

Useful words

sprain	to injure a joint by suddenly stretching or turning it
twist your ankle	to injure your ankle (= the joint between your leg and your foot) by suddenly turning it
a pharmacist	a person whose job is to prepare and sell medicines
a wheelchair	a chair with wheels that you use if you cannot walk very well

Could you tell me where the doctor's office is?
Could you tell me where to find the clinic?
Could you tell me your symptoms?

I'd like to know how long this will take.
I'd like to know where the eye department is.
I'd like to know what treatment you would recommend.

When you are speaking to a doctor or nurse, you may want to ask for advice. You can start your questions with **What's the best way ... ?**, **What would you recommend ... ?**, **What should I do ... ?**, or **Could you give me some advice about/on ... ?**

What's the best way to lose weight?
What's the best way of keeping my blood pressure under control?
What's the best way to treat depression?
What's the best way of keeping fit?

What would you recommend for a migraine?
What would you recommend for a bad cough?
What would you recommend for someone with the flu?
What would you recommend to keep his temperature down?

Useful words

a clinic	a place where people receive medical advice or treatment
a symptom	something that is wrong with you that is a sign of a particular illness
recommend	to suggest that someone would find something good or useful
lose weight	to become thinner
depression	a state of mind in which you are very sad, and you feel you cannot enjoy anything
a migraine	a very bad headache
flu	an illness that is like a very bad cold
a cough	when you suddenly force air out of your throat with a noise

What should I do if it happens again?
What should I do if it starts to bleed?
What should I do if the swelling gets worse?
What should I do if my children catch it?

Could you give me some advice about dieting?
Could you give me some advice about treating eczema?
Could you give him some advice on how to give up smoking?
Could you give him some advice about how to take the medicine?

Asking for things

When you want to find out if something is available, use **Do you have ... ?**

Do you have anything for a headache?
Do you have anything for hay fever?
Do you have the doctor's phone number?

If you want to ask for something, start your sentence with **Can I have ... ?**
To be very polite, use **please**.

Can I have an appointment for tomorrow, please?
Can I have a bottle of aspirin, please?
Can I please have a band-aid?

Useful words

bleed	to lose blood from a part of your body
swelling	an area that is larger and thicker than normal
your diet	the food that you regularly eat
eczema	a medical condition which causes red, dry areas of skin
an aspirin	a medicine used to reduce pain and fever
a band-aid	a small piece of sticky material that you use to cover small cuts on your body

If you want to buy something in a pharmacy, use **Can I have ... ?**, **I'd like ...** , or
I'm looking for ... .

> **I'd like** some cough medicine, please.
> **I'd like** a toothbrush for a child.

> **I'm looking for** soap.
> **I'm looking for** vitamins for pregnant women.
> **I'm looking for** something to help with my indigestion.

Can I ... ? is used in sentences where you are asking if something is allowed or
possible. If you want to be very polite, you can use **Is it possible ... ?**

> **Can I** see the dentist this morning?
> **Can I** drive while I'm taking this medicine?

> **Is it possible** to see a different doctor?
> **Is it possible** to meet the surgeon before my operation?

Useful words

a vitamin	a substance in food that you need in order to stay healthy
indigestion	pains in your stomach because of something that you have eaten
a surgeon	a doctor who is specially trained to do operations

If you are asking someone whether they can do something for you, you should use **Can you ... ?** or **Could you ... ?**, which is slightly more formal. To be very polite, you can use **please**. **Would you mind ... ?** is another polite way of asking someone to do something.

> **Can you** give me something for my earache, please?
> **Can you** send an ambulance straight away?
>
> **Could you** take us to the nearest hospital?
> **Could you** check my blood pressure?
>
> **Would you mind** changing this dressing for me?
> **Would you mind** passing me that bandage?

> **GOOD TO KNOW!**
> Notice that after **Would you mind** the verb always ends in -ing.

Saying what you want to do

A simple and polite way of saying what you want to do is by using **I'd like to ...** .

> **I'd like to** make an appointment with the doctor.
> **I'd like to** see a dentist as soon as possible.
> **I'd like to** talk to the pharmacist.

> **GOOD TO KNOW!**
> It is more polite to say **I'd like to** than **I want to**.

Useful words
a dressing   a covering that protects an injury

Use **I'd prefer to ...** or **I'd rather ...** when you want to do one thing more than another. When you use **I'd rather ...**, note that if you want to mention the thing that you do not want, you should use **than**.

> **I'd prefer to** see a female doctor.
> **I'd prefer to** have the operation next week.
> **I'd prefer** not **to** take antibiotics.

> **I'd rather** have a private room.
> **I'd rather** see a physical therapist.
> **I'd rather** take pills **than** get an injection.

You can talk about things that are important for you to do or to have by using **I need ...** .

> **I need** a prescription for my migraine pills.
> **He needs** to see a doctor right away.

Making suggestions

The simplest way to make a suggestion is to say **We could ...** or **Should we ... ?**

> **We could** get some tissues at the pharmacy.
> **You could** try to get an appointment tomorrow.

> **Should we** call a doctor?
> **Should we** put a bandage on it?

Useful words

antibiotics	drugs that are used for killing bacteria and curing infections
a physical therapist	someone whose job is to treat people who have injuries by moving parts of their body
an injection	medicine that is put into your body using a special needle
a prescription	a piece of paper on which a doctor writes an order for medicine
right away	as soon as possible
a tissue	a piece of thin, soft paper that you use to wipe your nose

Another way to make a suggestion is to say **Why don't ... ?** or **Why not ... ?**

> **Why don't** we ask for an appointment with a heart specialist?
> **Why don't** we ask the nurse for advice?
> **Why don't** you keep a diary of your symptoms?

> **Why not** see if you can take some time off work?
> **Why not** try an osteopath?
> **Why not** try cutting out milk from your diet?

How about ... ? is a slightly informal way of making suggestions of things to do or use.

> **How about** trying vitamins?
> **How about** changing your diet a little?
> **How about** walking to work instead of driving?

GOOD TO KNOW!
The verb that comes after **How about** must be in the -ing form.

Useful words

a specialist	a person who knows a lot about a particular subject
a nurse	a person whose job is to care for people who are sick
an osteopath	someone who treats injuries to bones and muscles
cut something out	to stop eating or drinking something
your diet	the type of food that you regularly eat

● Listen for

Here are some useful phrases you are likely to hear or use at the doctor's office, the clinic, or the hospital.

How are you?
What can I do for you?
How long have you been feeling this way?
Do you have any pre-existing medical conditions?
Are you on any other medication?
Do you feel sick?
Do you feel dizzy?
Where does it hurt?
Don't drink alcohol while you're taking this medicine.
Please fill out this form.
Can I see your insurance card?
The results look good.
Are you allergic to any antibiotics?

My throat is very sore.
I've been feeling nauseous.
I've got a sharp pain in my side.
I get out of breath easily.
I'm not sleeping well.
I have no appetite.
I'm getting a lot of headaches.

Listen to the conversation: Track 17

Brett has a skin problem and is asking a pharmacist for advice.

A I wonder if you can help me. I've got a problem with my skin. I have these sore patches behind my knees. They're dry and red, and they hurt if I touch them. Sometimes it gets so bad that I can't bend my legs.

B Do you mind if I take a look?

A Not at all.

B Hmm, yes. It looks like a small patch of eczema.

A Do you have anything for it?

B You could try this cream — it's pretty effective.

A How often should I put it on?

B Twice a day — once when you get up and again just before you go to bed.

A What about changing my diet? Would that help?

B Well, you could try cutting out dairy products for a while — sometimes that can help with eczema.

A Thanks, I'll try that. And what should I do if it doesn't get better?

B If it isn't better in a week or so, you should go and see your doctor.

 Listen to more phrases and practice saying them: Track 18

Help!

Don't worry!

If you find yourself in a situation in which you need help, for example if you have a problem, have an accident, or lose something, use the following phrases.

Describing the problem

If you are asking somebody for help, you will need to be able to describe the problem. Use **There is ...** to say what the problem is. If the problem is that you do not have something you need, use **There isn't ...** .

> **There's** water all over the floor.
> **There's** smoke coming out of the engine.
> **There are** mice in the kitchen.
>
> **There isn't** any soap in the bathroom.
> **There isn't** enough food for everyone.
> **There isn't** any gas in the car.

For some problems, you can use **I have ...** .

> **I have** a problem.
> **I have** a flat tire.
> **She has** too much luggage to carry.
> **I have** the wrong kind of plug for my laptop.

Useful words

smoke	the black or white clouds of gas that you see in the air when something burns
an engine	the part of a car that produces the power to make it move
gas	the fuel which you use in cars and some other vehicles to make the engine go
a towel	a piece of thick soft cloth that you use to dry yourself
flat	with not enough air inside
a tire	a thick round piece of rubber that fits around the wheels of cars and bicycles
luggage	the bags that you take with you when you travel
a plug	the plastic object with metal pins that connects a piece of electrical equipment to the electricity supply

If the problem is that you are not able to do something, use **I can't ...** .

> **I can't** turn the heat on.
> **I can't** get the car to start.
> **I can't** remember my password.
> **He can't** find his keys.

If you do not have the knowledge to do something, use **I don't know how to ...** .

> **I don't know how to** turn on the stove.
> **I don't know how to** get my email.
> **We don't know how to** get there.
> **I don't know how to** change a fuse.

If a piece of equipment will not do what you want it to do, use **The ... won't ...** .

> **The** engine **won't** start.
> **The** cable **won't** reach the socket.
> **The** barbecue **won't** light.
> **The** shower **won't** work.

Useful words

heat	the equipment that is used for keeping a building warm
a password	a secret word or phrase that allows you to use a computer system
a fuse	a small wire in a piece of electrical equipment that stops it from working when too much electricity passes through it
a cable	a thick wire that carries electricity
a socket	a hole that something fits into to make a connection
a barbecue	a piece of equipment that you use for cooking outdoors
light	to start something burning

Saying what happened

You will probably need to explain to somebody what happened. You can use **I ...** .

> I forgot my passport.
> I had an accident.
> **We** lost the key.
> **She** broke her glasses.

To describe what someone else has done to you, use **I was ...** . When you don't know the person who did it, use **Someone ...** .

> **I was** mugged.
> **We were** robbed.
> **We were** overcharged.
> **She was** attacked.

> **Someone** stole my camera.
> **Someone** broke into the apartment while we were out.
> **Someone** took my bag while we were having dinner.
> **Someone** hit me on the back of my head.

Describing people and things

The simplest way to describe things that have been lost or stolen is using **It's ...** .

> **It's** a black Honda with red seats.
> **It's** a gold ring with three diamonds.

Useful words

mug	to attack someone and steal their money
rob	to enter a building by force and steal things
overcharge	to charge someone too much for something
break in	to get into a building by force

When you are describing something, you may need to give more facts. Use **It's made of ...** to say what it is made of.

> It's a small bag, and **it's made of** velvet.
> The beads are bright blue, and **they're made of** glass.

To give more details about what something is like, use **It has ...** .

> **It has** a black handle.
> **It has** my name inside it.
> **They have** Chinese writing on them.

You may need to describe someone who is lost or has done something bad. Use **He/She has ...** to talk about what someone looks like.

> **She has** short blond hair.
> **He has** a beard.
> **She has** a small mouth.
> **They** both **have** brown eyes.

To talk about someone's clothes, use **He's/She's wearing ...** .

> **She's wearing** jeans and a green T-shirt.
> **She's wearing** an orange blouse.
> **He's wearing** a black jacket.
> **They're wearing** bathing suits.

Useful words

velvet	soft cloth that is thick on one side
a bead	a small piece of coloured glass, wood or plastic that is used for making jewellery
a handle	the part of a tool, a bag or a cup that you hold
blond	with pale-coloured hair
a blouse	a shirt for a girl or a woman
a bathing suit	a piece of clothing that you wear for swimming

Asking for information

You may need someone with a special skill to help you. Use **Is there ...** to ask about where to find that person. You may need to get someone's attention before you can ask them a question. Use **Excuse me** to do this.

> Excuse me, **is there** a garage near here?
> **Is there** a police station near here?

If you want to know where to go to get help with your problem, use **Where can I find ... ?**

> **Where can I find** someone to fix my watch?
> **Where can I find** information on how get oil stains out of clothes?
> **Where can I find** a good mechanic?

If you want someone to suggest someone or something that is good at fixing a problem, use **Can you recommend ... ?**

> **Can you recommend** a good dry cleaner?
> **Can you recommend** a plumber?
> **Can you recommend** a wood polish for a scratched floor?

Useful words

a garage	a place where you can have your car repaired
a police station	the local office of the police in a particular area
a stain	a mark on something that is difficult to remove
a mechanic	a person whose job is to repair machines and engines, especially car engines
a dry cleaner	a shop where things can be cleaned with a special chemical rather than with water
a plumber	a person whose job is to put in and repair water and gas pipes
polish	a substance that you put on a surface in order to clean it and make it shine

Use **Can you give me the number ...** to ask for the phone number of someone who can fix a problem.

> **Can you give me the number** of an electrician?
> **Can you give me the number** for the local police station?
> **Can you give me the number** of someone who can clean my chimney?

Asking for things

If you want to ask for something that will help with your problem, the simplest way is to use **Can I have ... ?**

> **Can I have** the phone number of an electrician?
> **Can I have** another form, please?

If you want to find out if something is available, use **Do you have ... ?**

> **Do you have** a fax machine?
> Excuse me, **do you have** a lost and found?
> Excuse me, **do you have** this document in English?

Useful words

an electrician	a person whose job is to repair electrical equipment
a chimney	a pipe above a fire that lets the smoke travel up and out of the building
a form	a piece of paper with questions on it and spaces where you should write the answers
lost property	things that people have lost or accidentally left in a public place

If you are asking someone whether they can do something for you, you should use **Can you ... ?** or **Could you ... ? Could you ... ?** is slightly more formal than **Can you ... ?** To be very polite, you can use **please**.

> **Can you** help me, **please**?
> **Can you** call the police?

> **Could you** recommend an electrician?
> **Could you please** show me how the shower works?

Use **Could I ... ?** when you want to ask if you can do something that will help you with your problem.

> **Could I** use your phone?
> **Could I** borrow a ladder, please?
> **Could I** pay you back later?

Saying what you want to do

The simplest way to say what you want to do about your problem is to use **I'd like to ...** . If you know that you do not want to do something, use **I don't want to ...** .

> **I'd like to** make a complaint.
> **I'd like to** make a call.

> **I don't want to** stay in this room.
> **I don't want to** leave my car here.

Useful words

recommend	to suggest that someone would find a particular person or thing good or useful
a ladder	a piece of equipment made of two long pieces of wood or metal with short steps that is used for reaching high places
a complaint	when you say that you are not satisfied

Use **I'd rather ...** when you want to do one thing more than another. If you want to mention the thing that you do not want, use **than**.

> **I'd rather** hire a lawyer who can speak English.
> **We'd rather** read the documents in English, if possible.
> **I'd rather** have my money back **than** be given a replacement.

Saying what you have to do

If it is important for you to do something, use **I have to ...** or **I need to ...** .

> **I have to** go to the American embassy.
> **I have to** leave my room by eleven.
> **I have to** tell my wife that we're safe.

> **I need to** speak to my lawyer.
> **I need to** make a call.
> **I need to** call an electrician.

Making suggestions

The most simple way to make a suggestion is to say **We could ...** or **Should we ... ?**

> **We could** borrow some money.
> **You could** try switching it off and on again.

> **Should we** call the police?
> **Should we** try to fix it ourselves?

Useful words

a lawyer	a person whose job is to advise people about the law
a replacement	a person or thing that takes the place of another
an embassy	the building where people who represent a foreign country work

Another way to make a suggestion is to say **Why don't ... ?** or **Why not ... ?**

Why don't we tie it with string?
Why don't we see what the police officer says?
Why don't you get a lift with Maria?

Why not see if the garage can fix the car today?
Why not see if you can get an earlier flight?
Why not ask Ben to lend you some tools?

> **GOOD TO KNOW!**
> **Why not + infinitive**
> The verb that comes after **Why not** must be in the base form.

Use **How about ... ?** if you have an idea about what to do about a problem.

How about asking the people in the store how it works?
How about getting a bank loan?
How about changing the oil?

> **GOOD TO KNOW!**
> **How about + -ing**
> The verb that comes after **How about** must be in the -ing form.

Useful words

tie	to fasten or fix something using string or a rope
string	very thin rope that is made of twisted threads
a lift	when you take someone somewhere in your car
a loan	an amount of money that you borrow

Talking about your plans

We often use **I'm + -ing verb** or **I'm going to ...** to talk about plans for dealing with problems.

> **I'm flying** out a day later than my husband.
> **I'm taking** it to the mechanic this afternoon.
> **We're seeing** our lawyer tomorrow.
> **We're changing** our phone service provider.

> **I'm going to** call the garage.
> **I'm going to** report the theft to the police.
> **I'm going to** call for help.
> **We're going to** ask him to pay for the damage.

Use **Are you going to ... ?** or **Will you ... ?** to ask someone about their plans.

> **Are you going to** tow our car?
> **Are you going to** let Juan know what happened?
> **Are you going to** change your ticket?
> **Are you going to** complain to the manager?

> **Will you** call us when it's ready?
> **Will you** fix the light at the same time?
> **Will you** charge extra for this?
> **Will you** be able to fix it?

Useful words

report	to tell people about something that happened
a theft	the crime of stealing
tow	to pull another vehicle along behind

● Listen for

Here are some key phrases you are likely to hear when you have some kind of problem.

What's the problem?
Is there anything I can do to help?
What was taken?
Can I have your address, please?
Can I see your driver's license?
Were there any witnesses?
Have you reported it to the police?
Can I have your insurance information?
Please fill out this form.

I have a problem that I need help with.
Do you have a number for a taxi company?
I need to get in touch with my husband right away.
There's been an accident.
My car broke down.
The shower/phone/radio doesn't work.
Could you fix my watch/shoes/bag?
Could you change the tire/oil?
Is there someone here who can speak English?

Useful words

a driver's license	a document that shows that you have passed a driving test and that you are allowed to drive
a witness	a person who saw an event such as an accident or a crime
insurance	an agreement that you make with a company in which you pay money to them regularly, and they pay you if something bad happens to you or your property
information	the facts about something
right away	as soon as possible
break down	to stop working

Listen to the conversation: Track 19

Emma's washing machine has broken down, and water is leaking everywhere. She calls her landlord to ask what to do.

A I have a problem with the washing machine. It suddenly stopped working, and now there's water all over the floor.

B OK, the first thing you have to do is turn the water supply off.

A I don't know how to do that.

B There's a tap behind the machine. Turn that off and then call a plumber.

A Can you recommend one?

B I always use Bob Wilbur.

A OK, can you give me his number?

B It's 562-4367.

A I'll call him right away.

B OK. I'll stop by this afternoon to help you clean up the mess.

Polly is on a business trip in Los Angeles. She has just heard that her mother is very ill, and in the hospital at home in New York. Polly is trying to get an early flight back.

A Excuse me, I have a problem that I need help with. I have a ticket to fly to New York on Saturday, but I just found out that my mother is very ill, and I need to get home as soon as possible.

B I'm sure we can help. There's a flight this afternoon at 1:55 and another one at 3 o'clock. Would you like me to check if there are any seats on those?

A That'd be great.

B Let's see. Yes, you're lucky — there's one seat left on the 3 o'clock flight.

A Oh, that's perfect, thanks! Could I have a vegetarian meal?

B I'm sorry, it's too late to change the food arrangements now.

A Oh, well. Thanks for your help.

 Listen to more phrases and practice saying them: Track 20

Calling and
writing

Getting in touch

Talking on the phone is one of the hardest things to do in a foreign language because you can't see the person you're speaking to, and you can't rely on body language and facial expressions to help you understand and communicate. This unit helps you to sound natural and confident when speaking on the telephone. It also shows you how to communicate by email, letter, or text.

Making a telephone call

If you want to tell someone that you need to make a phone call, use **I need to ...** .

> **I need to** make a call.
> Don't forget **you need to** call your mother back tonight.
> **I need to** charge my mobile.

To ask for a phone number, use **Do you have ... ?**

> **Do you have** his home number?
> **Do you have** the number of a taxi company?
> **Does she have** a mobile number?

You can also ask questions using **What ... ?**

> **What**'s her extension?
> **What**'s the code for the United States?
> **What** do I dial to get an outside line?

Useful words

a code	a group of numbers or letters that give information about something
an extension	a telephone that is connected to the main telephone in a building
dial	to press the buttons on a telephone in order to call someone
an outside line	a telephone line that connects you to someone outside the building you are in

When the person you're calling answers

Once you've made the call and someone answers, you will need to tell them who you are. Use **Hello, it's ...** .

>**Hello** Mr. Hall, **it's** Alex Ronaldson.
>**Hello**, is Stephanie in? **It's** Marie.

If the person you are calling does not know you, or know who you are, use **Hello, my name is ...** . To explain more about who you are, use **I'm ...** .

>**Hello, my name is** Rosie Green. **I'm** a colleague of Peter's.
>**Hello, my name is** Lorna McCall. **I'm** Tanya Hill's assistant.

To check that you are speaking to the right person, use **Is that ... ?**

>**Is this** Richard?
>**Is this** Dr. Kenyon's office?

If you want to ask for somebody, use **Is ... there?** or **Can I speak to ... ?**

>**Is** Oliver **there**?
>**Are** your parents **there**?

>**Can I speak to** the manager, please?
>**Can I speak to** whoever's responsible for road safety?

> **GOOD TO KNOW!**
> If the person you want to speak to is not there, you may be told **Sorry, he's not here** or **Sorry, she's not in.** If the person is there, you may be asked **Who's calling, please?** Answer by saying your name.

Useful words
an assistant   a person who helps someone in their work
a manager   a person who controls all or part of a business or organization
responsible   having the job or duty to deal with something

We often start a telephone conversation, especially with someone we know, by asking about their health, using **How are you?**

> Hello, Kendra. **How are you?**
> Hi, it's Chuck. **How are you?**
> **How's your brother?**

> **GOOD TO KNOW!**
> To answer that question, use **I'm fine, thanks** or **I'm good thanks.** If you are not well, you could say **Not great, really** or **Not too good, actually.**

You can start other general questions with **How's ... ?**

> **How's** life?
> **How are** things with you?
> **How's** your new job going?

Saying why you're calling

To say why you are calling, use **I'm calling about ...** or **I'm calling to ...** .

> **I'm calling about** your ad for programmers.
> **I'm calling about** Dad's birthday party.
> **I'm calling about** the ballet classes.

> **I'm calling to** make an appointment to have our carpet cleaned.
> **I'm calling to** find out whether you sell garden furniture.
> **I'm calling to** invite you and Stephanie over for dinner.

To explain where you are or what company or organization you are from, use **I'm calling from ...** .

Useful words

an ad	information that tells you about something such as a product, an event, or a job
ballet	a type of dancing that needs a lot of skill and in which there are carefully planned movements

I'm **calling from** the hotel.
I'm **calling from** the lawyer's office.
I'm **calling from** the charity Help our Horses.

If you want to ask whether you can do something, use **Can I ... ?**

Can I charge my phone here?
Can I use my cell inside?
Can I call him at work?

To ask someone else to do something, use **Could you ... ?**

Could you give her a message, please?
Could you put me through to Johanna, please?
Could you ask him to call me back?

Giving information

When you make a phone call, you may be asked to give your own phone number. Use **My number is ...** .

My home **number is ...**
...and **my** cellphone **number is ...**
My number at work **is ...**

Useful words	
a charity	an organization that collects money for people or animals that need help
charge something	to put electricity into something
put someone through	to connect someone to someone else on the telephone

To give details of where you can be contacted, use **You can contact me on ...** or **You can contact me at ...** .

> **You can contact me at** (617) 555-3264.
> **You can contact me on** my cell.
> **You can contact me at** my sister's number.

Answering the telephone

> **GOOD TO KNOW!**
> It is very common to say **Hello** when we answer the phone. At work, people sometimes answer by saying their name.

If the person who is calling asks for you, say **Speaking** or **This is ...** .

> "Can I speak to Lily?" "**This is Lily**."
> "Is Ms. Roberts there?" "**Speaking**."

To ask what the person calling wants to do, use **Would you like ... ?**

> **Would you like** to leave a message?
> **Would you like** me to ask him to call you back?
> She's on another call at the moment. **Would you like** to hold?

To ask the person calling to do something, use **Would you mind ... ?**

> **Would you mind** repeating that?
> **Would you mind** spelling your name, please?
> **Would you mind** calling back tomorrow?

Useful words

hold	to wait while still connected to the telephone until someone is free to speak to you
spell	to speak each letter of a word in the correct order

Ending a telephone call

When you end a telephone call, say **Goodbye** the same way you would if you were leaving someone. This is often shortened to **Bye.**

> Thanks for your help. **Goodbye**.
> OK then, **goodbye**.

> **Bye** Lynne! Talk to you later!
> **Bye**. See you soon.

To give someone good wishes for the next period of time, use **Have a good ... !**

> **Have a good** day!
> **Have a good** weekend!
> **Have a good** vacation!

When you say goodbye, you may want to say hello to someone else. In an informal situation, use **Say hello to ...** , and in a very formal situation, use **Give ... my best wishes.** .

> **Say hello to** your family.
> **Say hello to** your sister for me.

> **Give** your father **my best wishes**.
> **Give** Laura **my best**.

● Listen for

Here are some useful phrases you may hear when using the telephone.

> Who's calling, please?
> Who can I say is calling?
> Please hold.
> Hang on a minute, I'll get him.
> You've got the wrong number.
> Do you have the extension?
> His line is busy.
> I'll put you through.
> Please leave a message after the tone.
> All our operators are busy, please call back later.
> You're breaking up.
> Thanks for calling.

Useful words

hold the line	to wait on the phone
an extension	the number of a phone that is connected to a main phone in an organization
busy	already being used
put someone through	to connect you to someone else on the phone
an operator	a person who connects phone calls in a place such as an office or a hotel
break up	if a phone line breaks up, you cannot hear the voices clearly

Writing letters and emails

Here are some useful phrases for writing letters and emails, and some examples of both.

Dear Paul,
Hi, Marta!

Love, Naima
Lots of love, Charlotte

All the best, Amandeep

Regards, Minh
Best regards, Bella
Yours, Sujata

To: miriam@ntlworld.com
Cc:
Subject: party for Stefan

Hi Dora!
Just a quick note to ask if you have any ideas about what to do for Stefan's party. I was thinking of having it at my place, but I'm worried about disturbing the neighbors. Do you think I should rent a room somewhere?

Let me know what you think!

Miriam

GOOD TO KNOW!
When you say your email address, say **at** for @ and **dot** for. So Miriam's address is miriam at ntlworld dot com.

63 Mill Street
Seattle,
WA 98136 — Your address

February 14, 2012 — The date

Dear Hannah

Thanks for the birthday card, and for your letter
— your description of your brother falling in the
pool made me laugh out loud!

I'm glad things are working out so well for you in
Turkey. And that's one of the reasons I'm writing
— I have two weeks' vacation coming up, and I
was thinking of going to visit — what do you
think?!?!

If it's not convenient, let me know, but it would
be so great to see you and meet all your new
friends.

Write back soon!

Holly

PS Is there anything you want me to bring
from home?

Use **PS** to add something to the end of a letter

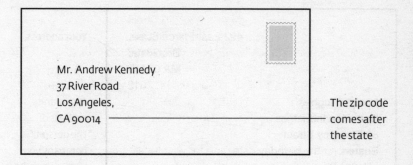

Mr. Andrew Kennedy
37 River Road
Los Angeles,
CA 90014

The zip code
comes after
the state

Starting a formal letter or email

Dear Mr. Surplice
Dear Prof. Amies
Dear Sir or Madam

> **GOOD TO KNOW!**
> Use **Dear Sir or Madam** or even something like **Dear Neighbors** or **Dear Parents**, depending on the reason you are writing.

Ending a formal letter or email

Yours truly, Anton Smith
Sincerely yours, Allie Sharpe

Ending a formal letter or email in a slightly more friendly way

Best wishes, Valerie Clark
Regards, Tony Bishop

492 East Pierce Street
Brookline,
MA 02445

Your address

Mrs. A. Hughes
Lawrence Industries
89 Chauncy Street
Boston,
MA 02111

Name and
address of
the person/
company you
are writing to

June 2, 2012

The date

Dear Mrs. Hughes,

I am writing to apply for the receptionist's job
advertised online.

I am currently working part-time as a
receptionist for a legal firm in Cambridge, but I
would like to find a full-time job.

I enclose my résumé and look forward to
hearing from you.

Sincerely yours,

Karen Miller

Karen Miller

Texting

Texting is a very popular and quick way to communicate. We often use special abbreviations for texting. Here are some common ones.

@	at	cul	see you later	sry	sorry
2	to *or* two	gr8	great	syl	see you later
2day	today	ic	I see	tx/thx	thanks
2moro	tomorrow	l8	late	u	you
4	for	l8r	later	w8	wait
aml	all my love	lol	laughing out	wan2	want to
b4	before		loud	wk	week
btw	by the way	m8	mate	wrk	work
c	see	pls	please	xlnt	excellent
cm	call me	r	are	y	why
cu	see you	some1	someone		

Listen to the conversation: Track 21

Jim is trying to get in touch with the finance manager of a large company.

A Good morning. Fletcher and Smith Finance. How can I help you?

B Could I speak to Ava Watts, please?

A Certainly. Who can I say is calling?

B My name is Jim Allsop. I'm calling from Franklin Printing.

A Thank you. I'll put you through. Oh, I'm sorry — Ms. Watts is on another line at the moment. Do you mind if I put you on hold?

B Hmm. Could you ask her to call me back?

A No problem. Can you give me your number?

B My office number is 718-555-7367, extension 56. If I'm not there, she can reach me on my cell — I think she has the number.

A Thank you very much. I'll give her the message.

B Thank you. Goodbye.

Emma is calling her friend Ashley.

A Hello.

B Hi, Ashley. It's Emma.

A Emma! Great to hear from you — how are things?

B Really good, thanks. I was calling to see if you want to come over and see my new apartment.

A I'd really love to, but I've got final exams next week, and then I'm moving myself.

B OK, I guess we'll have to wait a while. Will you still be at this number when you move?

A No, but you can call me on my cell.

B Well good luck on your finals.

A Thanks for calling. And say hello to Lara for me!

B I will. Bye for now.

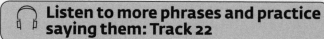

Listen to more phrases and practice saying them: Track 22

Work

At work

Whether you are discussing a project, making a telephone call to a customer or arranging a meeting at work, you will need to say a variety of things to your colleagues. These phrases will help you to talk naturally and confidently in a work situation.

Greetings

Many types of work involve meeting people that you do not know. To tell someone you have just met your name, use **Hello, I'm ...** .

> **Hello, I'm** Carlos Sanchez.
> **Hello, I'm** Lanying Peng.

If a person tells you their name, reply by saying **Pleased to meet you** or **Nice to meet you.** Then tell them your name by first saying **I'm ...** .

> **Pleased to meet you. I'm** Carole Durand.
> **Nice to meet you. I'm** Patricia Chapman.

You may also want to tell the person what your job is in the company. To do this, say **I'm ...** .

> **I'm** the marketing manager for Latin America.
> **I'm** the head of sales for Western Europe.
> **I'm** Director of Human Resources at Winters International.

Useful words

a customer	someone who buys something from a store or website
a colleague	a person someone works with
marketing	the advertising and selling of products
a manager	a person who controls all or part of a business or organization
a head	the person who is in charge of a company or organization
director	one of the people that controls a company or an organization
human resources	the part of a company that employs and trains people and deals with people who have problems

Introducing people

You may want to introduce a new person to a colleague. The simplest way to do this is to say **This is ...** giving the person's full name after.

> Leila, **this is** Chen Wang.
> Keisha, **this is** Anna-Maria Delgado. Anna-Maria, **this is**
>   Keisha Walker.

Another way of introducing two people, especially if you are not sure whether they have met before, is to start by saying **Have you met ... ?** If the two people have not met, you can then introduce them as above.

> Lucia, **have you met** Jin?
> Ed, **have you met** Sara? Sara, this is Ed Gooden.
> Carin, **have you met** Bruno? Bruno, this is Carin Williams.

Talking about your plans

When you are with your colleagues, you may want to talk about things that you will definitely do that day, that week, that month, etc. For plans like these that you are sure of, you can use **I'm + -ing verb**.

> **I'm seeing** a colleague here in half an hour.
> **She's attending** a conference in Madrid next week.
> **I'm meeting** Carlo and Scott tomorrow to discuss the issue.

Useful words

introduce	to tell people each other's names so that they can get to know each other
attend	to be present at an event
a conference	a long meeting about a particular subject
discuss	to talk about something
an issue	an important subject that people are talking about

For plans that you are sure of, you can also use **I'm going to ...** .

> **I'm going to** email Faisal this morning to let him know.
> **I'm going to** call the Beijing office today.
> **We're going to** meet Channa to talk about book sales.

To talk about your plans, you can also use **I plan to ...** or **My plan is to ...** .

> **I plan to** have the work finished by the end of next week.
> **I plan to** visit the Montreal office in June.
> **I plan to** hold a series of meetings to discuss the matter.

> **My plan is to** consult all the managers before making any decisions.
> **My plan is to** work on the report this Friday.
> **My plan is to** circulate the document among the managers first.

If you want to talk about a plan that you are not completely sure about, you can use **I hope to ...** .

> **I hope to** finish the report this week.
> **I hope to** meet with Celia while I'm in Mexico.
> **We hope to** complete the project by December 12th.

To talk about what should happen in the future, use **I'm supposed to ...** .

> **I'm supposed to** send the figures to Adam today.
> **I'm supposed to** speak at the conference.
> What time **are we supposed to** meet?
> **He's supposed to** call me this morning.

Useful words

a series	a number of things or events that come one after another
a matter	something that you must talk about or do
consult	to ask someone for their advice
a report	a piece of work that is written on a particular subject
circulate	to send something to all the people in a group
a document	a piece of text that is stored on a computer

Making suggestions

To say to a colleague that you will do something, use **I can ...** or **I'll ...** .

> **I can** check these figures.
> **I can** speak to Adriana, if you like.
> **I can** ask him, if you like.

> **I'll** order more stationery.
> **I'll** email Santiago, if you like.
> **I'll** send you a copy, if you like.

> **GOOD TO KNOW!**
> When people use **I can ...** or **I'll ...** to say they will do something, they often add **if you like**.

To suggest something that you and your colleagues could do, use **we could ...** .

> **We could** cancel the contract.
> **We could** refuse to pay them.
> **We could** offer the job to someone else.

Another way to suggest something that you and your colleagues could do is **Should we ... ?**

> **Should we** postpone the meeting?
> **Should we** discuss this with Natalia?
> **Should we** tell the staff?

Useful words

check	to make sure that something is correct
order	to ask for something to be sent you from a company
stationery	paper, envelopes, and other materials or equipment used for writing or typing
a copy	something that is produced that looks exactly like another thing
cancel	to say that something that has been planned will not happen
a contract	an official agreement between two companies or people
postpone	to arrange for an event to happen at a later time
staff	the people who work for an organization

Asking for suggestions

The simplest way of asking a colleague for advice is **Should I ... ?**

> **Should I** ask Domenico first?
> **Should I** send a copy of the letter to Lee?
> **Should I** forward this email to Hualing?

Another way of asking for advice is **Do you think I should ... ?**

> **Do you think I should** set up a meeting?
> **Do you think I should** tell my boss?
> **Do you think we should** hire someone else?

If you are asking a colleague whether they think something is good and should be used or done, say **Would you recommend ... ?**

> **Would you recommend** advertising in the paper?
> **Would you recommend** using their service?
> **Would you recommend** taking a client there for lunch?

Saying what you have to do

To tell your colleagues that it is very important that you do something, use **I have to ...** or **I need to ...** .

> **I have to** email Cyrus and ask him.
> I really **have to** finish this piece of work today.

Useful words	
forward	to send a letter or an email to someone after you have received it
set up something	to arrange something
a boss	the person in charge of you at the place where you work
hire	to pay someone to do a job for you
advertise	to tell people about something in newspapers, on television, on signs, or on the Internet
a service	the help that people in a shop, restaurant, or company give you
a client	a person who pays someone for a service

You have to call the customer when the goods are ready.

You don't **have to** work until eight o'clock every night.

I need to call our supplier.

I need to cancel that order.

We need to work more quickly.

To ask what someone has to do, use **Do you have to ... ?**

Do you have to work overtime?

Do you have to get to work by nine o'clock?

Do you have to have lunch with your colleagues?

Use **I should ...** to say what is the right thing to do, even if you are not going to do it.

I should call Doug and let him know.

I should offer her the job first.

We really **should** pay him the same as we pay Jamila.

Useful words

goods	things that you can buy or sell
a supplier	a company that sells something such as goods or equipment to customers
an order	the thing that someone has asked for
overtime	extra time that you spend doing your job
let someone know	to tell someone about something

> **GOOD TO KNOW!**
> There is no "to" after **I should ...** .

Asking for things

To ask a colleague if you can have something, use **Can I ... ?** or **Could I ... ?**
Could I ... ? is slightly more formal than **Can I ... ?** To be very polite, use **please**.

Can I use your cell, please?
Can I see those figures, please?
Can I to the meeting?

Could I please see that document?
Could I use your laptop?
Could I have a copy of that document?

To ask a colleague if they can do something for you, use **Can you ... ?** or **Could you ... ?**

Can you ask Jackie to call me, please?
Can you please take a message for me?
Can you get me those figures?

Could you send me that report?
Could you speak to Jingfei about the problem?
Could you please get the report to me by next Wednesday?

Useful words
a laptop   a small computer that you can carry with you

A very polite way to ask a colleague if they can do something for you is to use **Would you mind + -ing?**

> **Would you mind contacting** the suppliers?
> **Would you mind taking** the minutes at the next meeting?
> **Would you mind writing** an agenda for the meeting?

If it is important for you to have something, you can use **I need ...** .

> I really **need** the information now.
> **We need** a supplier that we can trust.
> We're so busy **we need** extra staff.

Apologizing

Sometimes when we are at work, there are problems and we make mistakes. When this happens, we may need to say we are sorry to a colleague or a customer. To apologize, use **I'm sorry ...** or **Sorry ...** .

> **I'm sorry** you didn't get the attachment with the email.
> **I'm sorry** I was late for the meeting.

> **Sorry** — I don't have a copy of the agenda.
> **Sorry**, I didn't hear what you were saying.

If you have to tell a colleague or a customer that there is a problem or that something bad has happened, start your sentence with **I'm afraid ...** .

> **I'm afraid** I can't come to the meeting.
> **I'm afraid** there's a problem with your order.

Useful words

contact	to call someone or send them an email, a message, or letter
take the minutes	to write what is said and decided at a formal meeting
an agenda	a list of things to be discussed at a meeting
busy	having a lot of things to do
an attachment	a file that is attached to an email message and sent with it

A very formal way of saying that you are sorry is to use **My apologies ...** .

> **My apologies** — I forgot to send you the memo.
> **My apologies** — my train was delayed.
> **My apologies** — that was my fault.

> **GOOD TO KNOW!**
> If someone apologizes to you, reply **That's all right** or **No problem**.
> This lets the person who is apologizing know that you are not angry
> with them or that the problem is not important.

Expressing opinions

If you want to give your opinion about something, use **I think ...** .

> **I think** their website is excellent.
> **I think** she's very good at giving presentations.
> **I don't think** they did a very good job.
> **I thought** she was the best candidate.

You can also give your opinion of something by saying **in my opinion ...** .

> **In my opinion**, these sales targets are too high.
> **In my opinion**, she's in the wrong job.

Useful words

a memo	a short note that you send to a person who works with you
delay	to make someone or something late
someone's fault	something bad that you have caused to happen
a website	a set of information about a particular subject that is available on the internet
a presentation	an occasion when someone shows or explains something to a group of people
a candidate	someone who is trying to get a particular job
a target	the result that you are trying to achieve

To ask someone for their opinion, say **What do you think of ... ?**

> **What do you think of** their products?
> **What do you think of** that strategy?

You can also ask someone for their opinion by saying **What's your opinion of ... ?**

> **What's your opinion of** the competition?
> **What's your opinion of** their performance?

Agreeing and disagreeing

If you think that what someone has said is right, say **I agree ...** .

> **I agree**. I think it's been a very successful project.
> Yes, **I agree** with you. We need to promote her.

You can also agree with what someone has said by saying **You're right ...** .

> **You're right.** Profits have declined.
> I think **you're right** about the website.

If you feel strongly that what someone has said is right, say **I totally agree ...** .

> **I totally agree**. I think she's an excellent leader.
> **I totally agree** with you, James.

Useful words

a strategy	a general plan or set of plans for the future
the competition	the company or person that you are competing against
a performance	how well someone does something
successful	doing or getting what you wanted
promote	to give someone a more important job in the same organization
a profit	the amount of money that you gain when you sell something for more money than you paid for it
decline	to become less in amount
a leader	the person who is in charge of a group of people or an organization

If you think that what someone has said is wrong, say **I disagree ...** .

> **I disagree**. I've always found her to be very efficient.
> **I disagree** with you here.
> I'm afraid I **disagree**.

If you feel strongly that what someone has said is wrong, say **I totally disagree ...** .

> **I totally disagree**. I think we've spent too much already on this project.
> I'm afraid I **totally disagree** with you.

> **GOOD TO KNOW!**
> When people say **I disagree**, they often start the sentence with
> **I'm afraid**.

● Listen for

Here are some important phrases you are likely to use and hear at work.

> We need to arrange a meeting to discuss this.
> Susan sends her apologies.
> Could someone take the minutes for the meeting?
> What's next on the agenda?
> Could you put together an agenda for the meeting?

> How do you turn this on?
> Where can I plug this in?
> My computer crashed again.
> I'll just start up my computer.
> I don't have any record of that.
> I forgot my password.

Useful words

efficient	able to do tasks successfully, without wasting time or energy
put together	to organize something
a password	a secret word or phrase that allows you to enter a place or use a computer system

Could you forward me that email?
I sent it as an attachment.
I can't open the attachment.
Could I talk to you?
Do you have a moment?
I'll have a word with him.

She applied for another job.
She's leaving the company.
He's been promoted.
He resigned.
She's retiring at the end of the year.

Useful words

a moment	a short amount of time
have a word with someone	to speak to someone
apply	to write a letter or write on a form in order to ask for something such as a job
resign	to tell your employer that you are leaving
retire	to leave your job and usually stop working completely

Listen to the conversation: Track 23

Annabel is telling her colleague Peter about a business trip that she is planning. It will be the first time she has traveled on business. Peter has traveled a lot.

A So where are you going?

B I'm meeting clients in New York, and then I'm going to Philadelphia for a conference.

A Where are you staying in New York?

B In midtown, if I can find a hotel that's not too expensive — and not booked up. I think that might be difficult at this time of the year.

A Could be. I can give you the names of a couple of places where I've stayed before. I'll email you the addresses when I get back to my desk.

B Oh, thanks, that would be great. Would you recommend meeting clients in the hotel itself — or should I find a place somewhere where we can meet?

A I don't think it matters. You just need to find somewhere quiet where you can sit down and talk without being disturbed.

B That makes sense. Anyway, I have to make reservations pretty soon. I'm leaving in three weeks.

A Just out of curiosity, who are you meeting in New York?

B A couple of people — Sharon Lopez and Kevin Hanks. Do you know them?

A Actually, I do.

B That's interesting. What do you think of Kevin?

A He's all right, but you have to be kind of tough with him. He tends to get what he wants out of a meeting.

B You're making me nervous! Do you think I should practice what I'm going to say?

A Yes, why not?

B If you have a couple of minutes later this week, would you mind listening to me?

A Not at all — I'd be happy to. How about this afternoon? I'm free after 3 o'clock. Just give me a call when you're ready.

B That'd be fantastic. Thanks a lot.

> **Listen to more phrases and practice saying them: Track 24**

studying

Academic life

If you are in school or college, the phrases in this section will help you to talk about your studies. You will be able to use them in discussions, to find information you need, and to express your opinions about the subjects you are studying.

Asking for information

When you need to get information about something, make questions with words such as **What ... ?, Where ... ?,** or **When ... ?**

> **What** are we studying this semester?
> **What** room is the lecture in?
> **Where** is the gym?
> **Where** can I get a library card?
> **When** is your first lecture?
> **When** do we have to hand in our essays?

A polite way to ask for general information is **Could you tell me ... ?**

> **Could you tell me** where Professor Lyman's office is, please?
> **Could you tell me** how to use this microscope?
> **Could you tell me** what time the library opens?

Useful words	
a lecture	a talk that someone gives in order to teach people about a particular subject
a gym	a club, building, or large room with equipment for doing physical exercises
hand something in	to take something to someone and give it to them
an essay	a short piece of writing on a subject
a microscope	a scientific instrument that makes very small objects look bigger

Use **Is there ... ?** or **Are there any ... ?** to ask whether something exists. You use these phrases especially when you want to have something to use.

> **Is there** any paper left?
> **Is there** a spare laptop here?
> **Are there** any pens in that box?
> **Are there** any more calculators?

A very common way of asking how to do something is to use the phrase **How do you ... ?** You could also say **What's the best way ... ?**

> **How do you** spell that?
> **How do you** divide a small number by a bigger number?
> **How do you** turn this computer on?

> **What's the best way** to improve my English pronunciation?
> **What's the best way** to prepare for the exam?
> **What's the best way** of recording the results of our experiment?

If you want to ask someone for advice about your studies, use **Could you give me some advice ... ?** This phrase is followed by the prepositions **about** or **on**.

> **Could you give me some advice** about what I should be reading?
> **Could you give me some advice** on how to organize my essay?
> **Could you give me some advice** about the best way to review for the test?

Useful words

spare	not being used by anyone else
a calculator	a small electronic machine that you use to calculate numbers
pronunciation	the way that you say a word
review	when you study something again in order to prepare for an exam

Expressing opinions

You will probably be asked to give your opinions about things you are studying. The simplest way is to use **I think ...** .

> **I think** this reading list is out of date.
> I really **think** that the only way to learn a language well is to live in the country.
> **I don't think** that's the correct answer.

You can also use **In my opinion ...** . This is a strong way to express your opinion, and is more suitable in a formal discussion in class than with friends.

> **In my opinion**, technology is a force for good.
> **In my opinion**, soccer is the most exciting sport.
> **In my opinion**, people should read more books.

To talk about someone else's opinion, you can use **According to ...** . This phrase is also more suitable in a formal discussion in class than with friends. You could also use **Some people say ...** , which is less formal.

> **According to** Virginia Woolf, every woman needs a room of her own.
> **According to** the latest research, genes play an important role in the disease.
> **According to** my teacher, the exam is more difficult now than it used to be.

Useful words

a reading list	a list of books on a particular subject that students are asked to read
research	when someone studies something and tries to discover facts about it
a gene	the part of a cell that controls a person's, an animal's, or a plant's physical characteristics, growth, and development
a role	what someone or something does in a situation

> **GOOD TO KNOW!**
> When you use **According to ...,** we do not say "According to me."

Some people say that Shakespeare did not really write all those plays.
Some people say Cisnero's best book is "The House on Mango Street."
Some people say Mozart was the greatest composer who ever lived.

If you want to ask other people their opinion of something, use **What do you think of ... ?** or **What do you think about ... ?**

What do you think of the new language labs?
What do you think of his book on Kennedy?

What do you think about Rivera's use of color in this painting?
What do you think about setting up a French conversation group?

To agree with someone's opinion, use **I agree** or **You're right**. If you want to say who you agree with, use **with**.

"This book is really informative." "**I agree**. I used it a lot when I was writing my essay."
I agree with Ana that we need more help with our experiment.
I completely **agree with** you!

"I think this chemical is sulphur." "**You're right**."
He's right that business studies is a useful subject.

Useful words

a composer	a person who writes music
a language lab	a room containing equipment for learning languages
informative	giving you useful information
sulphur	a yellow chemical that has an unpleasant smell
business studies	the study of how businesses work

If you do not agree with someone, you can use **I don't agree, I'm afraid I don't agree,** or **I don't really agree.**

> "What a great lecture." "**I don't agree**. She didn't tell us anything new."
> "I think Washington was the greatest leader in American history."
> "**I'm afraid I don't agree.** For me, it has to be Lincoln."
> "Media studies is just a waste of time." "**I don't really agree.** It teaches you a lot about analyzing what you see."

Another way of saying that you do not agree is **I disagree.**

> "I.M. Pei is the most interesting architect of the 20th century."
> "**I disagree**. What about Gaudi?"
> "He says most people are honest." "Well, **I disagree** with him on that."
> "Churchill was Britain's greatest Prime Minister." "I strongly **disagree**."

Asking for and giving explanations

You will often need to ask your teacher to explain things. The simplest way is to use **Why ... ?**

> **Why** do we need protein in order to grow?
> **Why** can't we use calculators?
> **Why** did the Egyptians build pyramids?

Useful words

media studies	the study of newspapers, televisions, advertising, etc.
analyze	to consider something carefully in order to fully understand it or to find out what is in it
admire	to like and respect someone or something very much
honest	always telling the truth and not stealing or cheating
the prime minister	the leader of the government in some countries
protein	a substance that the body needs that is found in meat, eggs, fish and milk
a calculator	a small electronic machine that you use to calculate numbers
a pyramid	a solid shape with a flat base and flat sides that form a point where they meet

Could you explain ... ? can be used to ask your teacher to explain something. Your teacher might use it to ask you to explain something, too.

> **Could you explain** how a liquid can change into a gas?
> **Could you explain** how volcanos are formed?
> **Could you explain** how it happened?
> **Could you explain** why you came to this conclusion?

Another way of asking for an explanation is **Why is it that ... ?**

> **Why is it that** we're not studying Frida Kahlo?
> **Why is it that** the glacier doesn't melt?
> **Why was it that** they lost that battle?

The simplest way of giving an explanation is to use **Because ...** .

> Many people died because penicillin hadn't been discovered yet.
> Your answer was wrong **because** you put the decimal point in the wrong place.
> **Because** heat cannot pass from a colder object to a warmer object.

Useful words

a volcano	a mountain that throws out hot liquid rock and fire
a conclusion	a decision that you make after thinking carefully about something
a glacier	a very large amount of ice that moves very slowly, usually down a mountain
a battle	a fight between armies during a war
a decimal point	the dot that you use when you write a number as a decimal

You can also use **The reason is that ...** .

> **The reason is that** trees absorb the carbon dioxide.
> **The reason is that** the second number is larger than the first.
> **The reason is that** mountains formed a natural barrier between them.

Explaining a problem

To explain a general problem, use **I have a problem ...** . Use the preposition **with** to talk about a thing that is causing your problem.

> **I have a problem** — I want to take a French class and a history class, but the classes are at the same time.
> **I have a problem with** my essay — it's too long, and I don't know what to cut out.
> **I have a problem with** my laptop.

To talk about something that has happened that is causing you a problem, use **I** with the past tense.

> **I lost** my notes.
> **I forgot** to bring my homework.
> **I messed up** the experiment.

If someone else has caused your problem, use **Someone** with the past tense.

> **Someone spilled** coffee all over my essay.
> **Someone stole** my laptop.

Useful words

absorb	to take in a substance
carbon dioxide	a gas that animals and people produce when they breathe out
a barrier	a fence or a wall that prevents people or things from moving from one area to another

If you do not know how to do something, use **I don't know how to ...** .

> **I don't know how to** measure the flow of electricity.
> **I don't know how to** set up the equipment.
> **I don't know how to** find the original reference.

If your problem is that you do not have something that you need, use **There isn't ...** or **There aren't ...** .

> **There isn't** a projector in this room.
> **There wasn't** enough time to ask questions.
> **There aren't** enough handouts for everyone.
> **There weren't** any aprons in the closet.

Asking for permission

The simplest way to ask your teacher or lecturer for permission to do something is to use **Can I ... ?**

> **Can I** send you a draft of my essay?
> **Can I** use this microscope?
> **Can we** look at the answers now?

Useful words

flow	when something moves somewhere in a steady and continuous way
set something up	to start or arrange something
original	used for talking about something that existed at the beginning
a reference	the name of the person who said or wrote something and the place where they said or wrote it
a projector	a machine that shows films or pictures on a screen or on a wall
a handout	a piece of paper containing information that is given to people in a meeting or a class
an apron	a piece of clothing that you wear over the front of your normal clothes, especially when you are cooking, in order to prevent your clothes from getting dirty

To ask if your teacher is happy for you to do something, use **Is it OK ... ?** or **Do you mind if ... ?**

> **Is it OK** to send my report as an email attachment?
> **Is it OK** to write in the margin?
> **Is it OK** if my report is longer than that?
>
> **Do you mind if** we go and work in the library?
> **Do you mind if** we miss the next class?

You could also see if something is allowed by using **Are we allowed to ... ?**

> **Are we allowed to** work in pairs?
> **Are we allowed to** retake the exam if we fail?

Saying what you like, dislike, prefer

The simplest way to talk about things you like is to use **I like ...** . To talk about activities that you like doing, use **I enjoy ...** .

> **I like** to read novels in the original language if I can.
> **I like** math.
>
> **I enjoy** researching new topics.
> I really **enjoy** the work.

Useful words

the margin	the empty space down the side of a page
a pair	two people who are doing something together
retake an exam	to take an exam again
a novel	a long written story about imaginary people and events
research	to study something and try to discover facts about it

> **GOOD TO KNOW!**
> **Like/Enjoy + -ing**
> When **like** or **enjoy** is followed by a verb, the verb is usually in the -ing form.

To tell someone what you do not like, use **I don't like ...** , or to make your view stronger, **I hate ...** .

> **I don't like** wasting time.
> **I don't like** physics.
>
> **I hate** being late for class.
> I really **hate** working in the library.

A slightly formal way of saying what you don't like is **I dislike ...** .

> **I dislike** having to read aloud in class.
> **I dislike** the atmosphere in her class.
> **She disliked** the professor's approach to the research.

If you want to say that you like one thing more than another, use **I prefer ...** . If you want to talk about the thing you like less, use **to**.

> **I prefer** history.
> **She prefers** studying in a group.
> **I prefer** to study on my own.

Useful words

the atmosphere	the general feeling that you get when you are in a place
approach	the particular way you deal with a task, problem, or situation

To say that you would prefer to do something, use **I'd rather ...** . If you want to talk about the thing you like less, use **than**.

> **I'd rather** use the library **than** carry so many books around with me.
> **I'd rather** give up math and concentrate on science.
> **We'd rather** take the exam online.

Talking about your plans

If you have decided what you are going to do, you could use **I'm going to ...** or **I'm planning to ...** .

> **I'm going to** ask Dr. Levy for some advice.
> **I'm going to** take a philosophy class this semester.
> **I'm going to** finish my dissertation this week.

> **I'm planning to** stay at home tomorrow and revise.
> **I'm planning to** go to culinary school.
> **I'm planning to** take a year off after school.

Useful words

concentrate on something	to give something all your attention
philosophy	the study of ideas about the meaning of life
a term	one of the periods of time that a school, college or university year is divided into
a dissertation	a long piece of writing on a subject you are studying
revise	to study something again in order to prepare for an exam
a culinary school	a school that teaches cooking for professionals

If you are considering doing something, you could use **I'm thinking of ...** .

> **I'm thinking of** taking a year off.
> **I'm thinking of** changing my major.
> **I'm thinking of** taking an economics class.

> **GOOD TO KNOW!**
> **I'm thinking of + -ing**
> The verb that follows **I'm thinking of** must be in the -ing form.

To talk about something that you would like to do but you are not sure if it is possible, use **I'm hoping to ...** .

> **I'm hoping to** study abroad.
> **I'm hoping to** go to Harvard.
> **I'm hoping to** study business.

You can also use **I'm supposed to ...** to show that there is some doubt about a plan.

> **I'm supposed to** hand this in today.
> **I'm supposed to** be in class now.
> **I'm supposed to** give a presentation to the class.

To ask someone about their plans, use **Are you going to ... ?**

> **Are you going to** major in French?
> **Are you going to** work harder this semester?
> **Are you going to** go to the library later?

Useful words

a presentation	an occasion when someone shows or explains something to a group of people
major in	to study one main subject

● Listen for

Here are some useful phrases you are likely to hear at school or college.

Turn to page 10.
Open your books to page 56.
Work in pairs/groups of 4.
Look it up in your dictionary.
Hand in your homework at the end of class.
Make sure you read the questions carefully.
Put the equipment away when you finish using it.
Make sure you check all your references.
Label your diagram.
Make sure your essay has a clear conclusion.
Write up the results of your experiments later today.
You must include a bibliography.

Useful words

look something up	to find a fact or piece of information by looking in a book or on a computer
a reference	a writer or a piece of work that you talk about in your writing
label	to write on something to explain what it is
a diagram	a simple drawing of lines
the conclusion	the part of an essay that shows your opinion about the subject
write up something	to write something using notes you made earlier
a bibliography	a list of the books you have used in your writing

Listen to the conversation: Track 25

Susie is talking to her advisor about what subjects to take next year.

A Could you give me some advice about what subjects to take next year? I really like art, and I'd love to continue with it, but I'm worried that it takes up too much of my time. I'm hoping to major in politics and economics, so I wonder if I should drop art.

B I understand that art takes a lot of your time. But in my opinion, if you love it enough, you'll find the time. But what about math? If you're going to study economics, you'll have to take several math classes.

A I have a problem with math — I just find it really difficult. I'd rather not take it if I don't have to.

B Well, that could be a problem. Is there a reason why you want to study economics? Why not major in politics on its own, or with something else — a language for instance?

A That's a good idea. What's the best way to find out what classes are available?

B All that information is on the school's website.

A OK, I'll do that. Thanks for your help.

 Listen to more phrases and practice saying them: Track 26

Numbers, dates, and time

Three, two, one... Go!

You will often need to use numbers in conversation. You will also need to talk about the time and dates. The phrases in this unit will help you to talk about all these things with confidence.

Numbers

To say how much something costs using the unit of money that is written as €, use **... euros** and for the smaller unit used with the euro, use **... cents**. For the unit of money that is written as £, use **... pounds** and for the smaller unit used with the pound, use **... pence**.

> It cost me sixty-five **euros** twenty. (€65.20)
> That'll be eighteen **euros** and ninety-nine **cents**. (€18.99)
> At twenty-nine **dollars** each ($29), the price is very reasonable.
> He bought a bar of chocolate for eighty-nine **pence**. (89p)
> My ticket cost nine **pounds** fifty-nine. (£9.59)
> It was going to cost three hundred **pounds** (£300), which I couldn't afford.

To talk about how heavy something is using the units of measurement written as k and g, use **... kilos** and **... grams**. To talk about how heavy something is using the units of measurement written as lb. and oz. use **... pounds** and **... ounces**.

> I'd like two **kilos** of potatoes, please.
> Can I have half a **kilo** of tomatoes?
> You need three **pounds** of apples.
> The recipe says eight **ounces** of butter.

Useful words

reasonable	not too high
can afford something	to have enough money to pay for something
a recipe	a list of food and a set of instructions telling you how to cook something

To talk about how much liquid there is using the unit of measurement written as L or l, use **... liters**. For the unit of measurement written as p or pt, use **... pints**.

> I put twenty **liters** of gas in the car yesterday.
> You need half a **liter** of milk for this recipe.
> Could you buy two **pints** of milk, please?

To talk about how long something is, using the units of measurement written as km, m and cm, use **... kilometers, ... meters,** and **... centimeters**. For the units of measurement written as m., yd., ft. and in., use **... miles, ... yards, ... feet,** and **... inches**.

> We're thirty **kilometers** from Madrid.
> I'm one **meter** sixty-six **centimeters** tall.
> It's twenty **centimeters** long by ten wide.
> It's about eighty **miles** to Dallas.
> He's over six **feet** tall.

To talk about amounts as parts of a hundred (%), use **... percent**.

> Fifty-five **percent** of the students are from the U.S.
> The rate of inflation is two point five **percent**.
> Sixty-eight **percent** of the population own their own homes.

For talking about a temperature, written as °, use **... degrees**.

> It's over thirty **degrees C** in the shade today.
> It's only one or two **degrees** above zero.
> It's two or three **degrees** hotter today.

Useful words

a rate	how fast or how often something happens
inflation	a general increase in the prices of goods and services in a country
population	all the people who live in a country or an area
shade	an area where direct sunlight does not reach

To talk about the order in which something happens or comes, use **first, second, third,** etc ... .

> We're celebrating our **first** wedding anniversary today.
> This is my **second** trip to this region.
> He came in **third** in the race.
> This is the **sixth** time I've eaten here.

The time

Use **... o'clock** to say what time it is when the clock shows the exact hour.

> He got up this morning at five **o'clock**.
> It's one **o'clock** — time for lunch!
> It's four **o'clock** in the afternoon.
> We're leaving at eight **o'clock** tomorrow morning.

> **GOOD TO KNOW!**
> **Noon** is used to mean twelve o'clock in the middle of the day.
> **Midnight** is used to mean twelve o'clock in the middle of the night.

To say that it is thirty minutes or less after a particular hour, use **... past ...** or **after** ... .

> It's twenty-five **past** one.
> It's five **after** six.
> It's quarter **after** one.
> She's coming here at half **past** five.

Useful words	
celebrate	to do something enjoyable for a special reason
an anniversary	a date that is remembered because something special happened on that date in an earlier year
a trip	a journey that you make to a particular place and back again
a region	an area of the country or of the world
a race	a competition to see who is the fastest

To say that it is a particular number of minutes before a particular hour, use **... to ...** .

> It's now twenty **to** one.
> It's ten **to** eight.
> I glanced at my watch, and it was five **to** three.
> We landed in Cairo at quarter **to** one.

To find out the time now or the time that something starts, use **What time ... ?**

> **What time** is it?
> Do you know **what time** it is?
> Could you tell me **what time** it is?
> **What time**'s the next train to Providence?
> **What time** is the next performance?

To say the time that something is happening, use **at ...** .

> The lecture starts **at** seven o'clock.
> The train leaves **at** seven thirty.
> I'll see you **at** half past three.
> Let's meet **at** quarter after five.

To say that something will happen at or before a particular time, use **by ...** .

> Can you be there **by** three o'clock?
> I have to leave **by** quarter to one.
> We have to finish this **by** quarter to two.

Useful words

glance	to look at someone or something very quickly
land	used for saying that a plane comes down to the ground
a performance	when you entertain an audience by singing, dancing or acting
a lecture	a talk that someone gives in order to teach someone about a particular subject
meet	to come together with someone, having planned to do this

● Listen for

Here are some important phrases you may hear and use to do with the time.

> Excuse me, do you have the time?
> It's probably about eleven.
> I'm in a hurry.
> I have to go — I'm late already.
> We're running out of time.
> Stop wasting time!
> Did you get there on time?
> How much time do we have left?
> He should be here by now.

> The train for Paris leaves at 13:55.
> The train to 4:15 Dayton will depart from Platform Two.
> Flight number 307 for London is due to take off at 2:45.
> Flight 909 from Toronto is on time.

Saying how long

If you want to say that something will happen in so many minutes' time or in so many days' time, use **in ...** .

> I'll be back **in** twenty minutes.
> She'll be here **in** a week.
> He completed the exercise **in** only three minutes.
> I can probably do the job **in** an hour or two.

Useful words	
in a hurry	needing or wanting to do something quickly
run out of something	to have no more of something left
waste	to use too much of something, such as time, doing something that is not important
on time	not late or early
due	expected to happen or arrive at a particular time
take off	used for saying that a plane leaves the ground and starts flying
an exercise	an activity that you do in order to practice a skill

To ask how much time something lasts or how much time you need for something, use **How long ... ?**

> **How long**'s the movie?
> **How long** does the meeting usually last?
> **How long** will the tour take?

To say how much time is needed to do something, use **It takes ...** .

> **It takes** five minutes to make.
> **It took** two hours to get there.
> **It took** three hours by train.

The seasons

To say which season, (spring, summer, autumn, or winter), something happens or happened in, use **in ...** .

> The weather is really beautiful **in** spring.
> We don't go camping **in** winter.
> They got married **in** the summer of 2009.
> They emigrated **in** autumn.

To make it clear which spring, summer, etc. you are talking about, use **last ...** , **this ...**, or **next ...** .

> I'm going to South Africa **this** winter.
> It was quite mild **last** winter.
> She's expecting her fifth baby **next** spring.

Useful words

a tour	a trip to an interesting place or around several interesting places
reach	to arrive at a place
camping	the activity of staying somewhere in a tent
get married	to legally become husband and wife in a special ceremony
emigrate	to leave your own country and go to live in another country
mild	not too cold
expect a baby	to have a baby growing inside you

208 numbers, dates, and time

The months of the year

To say which month of the year something happens or happened in, use **in ...** .

> The twins have their birthday **in** August.
> We'll probably take our vacation **in** May.
> I visited some friends in Rome **in** September.
> We're going to the coast **in** August.

To make it clear which January or February, etc. you are talking about, use **last ...** , **this ...**, or **next ...** .

> What are you doing **this** summer?
> Are you going abroad **this** summer?
> We went to Hawaii **last** June.
> I'm hoping to go to South America **next** July.

If you want to say which part of a month something happens in, use **at the beginning of ...**, **in the middle of**, ... or **at the end of ...** .

> She starts school **at the beginning of** September.
> Summer vacation start **at the end of** June.
> They're moving **in the middle of** November.

Useful words

a twin	one of two people who were born at the same time to the same mother
the coast	the land that is next to the sea
abroad	in or to a foreign country
move	to go to live in a different place

Dates

To say what the date is, use **the first/second, etc. of March/November, etc.**
or **March/November, etc. first/second, etc.**

>It's **the first of July** today.
>Tomorrow**'s the tenth of January**.
>Today's **December third**.
>Next Monday will be **March fifth**.

To say what date something is happening or happened on, use **on ...** before
the date.

>He was born **on** the fourteenth of February, 1990.
>We got engaged **on** April twenty-third.
>Barbara and Michael got married **on** May fifteenth.
>Where do you think you'll be **on** the twentieth of October?

GOOD TO KNOW!
To ask what the date is, use **What's today's date?**

The days of the week

To say what day of the week it is, use **It's** or **Today's ...** .

>"What day is it?" "**It's** Thursday."
>**Today's** Wednesday, isn't it?
>Great! **It's** Saturday.

When saying which day something happens or will happen, use **on ...** .

>I'm seeing the consultant **on** Thursday.
>It's my birthday **on** Tuesday.
>We'll see them **on** Wednesday.
>I don't work **on** Fridays.

Useful words

get engaged	to agree to marry someone
a consultant	someone who gives expert advice on a subject

To say what time of a particular day something happens, use **on ... morning/ afternoon/evening/night**.

> I'm going to see the real estate agent **on Tuesday morning**.
> I'll see you **on Friday afternoon**.
> There was a good movie on TV **on Sunday evening**.
> What are you doing **on Saturday night**?

To say that you do something all Mondays/Saturdays, etc. use **every ...** .

> We call her **every** Monday.
> He plays golf **every** Saturday.
> I used to see them **every** Friday.
> They go to the same café **every** Saturday morning.

To say that you do something one Wednesday/week, etc. and then not the next Wednesday/week, etc., and that it continues in this way, use **every other ...** .

> He has the children **every other** weekend.
> We play football **every other** Saturday.
> Danielle and I have coffee together **every other** Friday after work.
> **Every other** Sunday, we volunteer at the clinic.

To make it clear which Monday/Wednesday, etc. you are talking about, use **last ... , this, ...** or **next ...** .

> It's our wedding anniversary **this** Friday.
> I'm going on vacation **this** Tuesday.
> I had a job interview **last** Friday.
> Would **next** Friday be better for you?

Useful words

a real estate agent	a person whose job is to sell buildings or land
a couple	two or around two people or things
volunteer	to offer to do something without being paid
an interview	a formal meeting in which someone asks you questions to find out if you are the right person for a job

If you want to ask what day something is happening, use **What day ... ?**

>**What day**'s the meeting? Is it Tuesday?
>**What day** is the bed being delivered?
>Do you know **what day** he's coming?
>I don't even know **what day** they're arriving.

To talk about a particular time the day after today, use **tomorrow ...** .

>I've got to be up early **tomorrow** morning.
>She leaves for Pusan **tomorrow** afternoon.
>I'm seeing her **tomorrow** evening.
>We're going to a party **tomorrow** night.

To talk about a particular time the day before today, use **yesterday ...** .

>It all happened **yesterday** morning while I was at work.
>He called at some point **yesterday** morning.
>I saw him in town **yesterday** afternoon.
>I heard my neighbors fighting **yesterday** evening.

GOOD TO KNOW!
To talk about the night that belonged to yesterday, you use **last night** and not **yesterday night**.

Useful words

deliver	to take something to a particular place
up	not in bed
a point	a particular time
a neighbor	someone who lives near you

To say when something happened, use **... ago**.

> She called me a week **ago**.
> Gina and Alessandro left ten days **ago**.
> He was born three years **ago**.
> I read his novel, but that was ages **ago**.

To say how long something has been happening, use **for ...** .

> It's been raining **for** five days
> I haven't seen them **for** three weeks.
> They haven't spoken to each other **for** months.
> She'd been waiting **for** over an hour and was a bit fed up.
> We've been living here **for** ten years now, and we both feel it's time for a change.
> I haven't seen her **for** a week and I'm starting to feel a little concerned.

GOOD TO KNOW!
Another way to say "for a long time" is **for ages**.

Useful words

a novel	a long written story about imaginary people and events
ages	a long time
fed up	annoyed or bored
concerned	worried

● Listen for

Here are some important phrases you may hear and use to do with dates, months of the year, days of the week, and seasons.

When's your birthday?
Today's my birthday!
It's my parents' wedding anniversary today.
When are you getting married?
When are you going on vacation?
When do you start classes?
When are you going to Rio?
When do you come back from Rio?
When is the baby due?
When was Carlo born?
When do you play tennis?
Which days are you free?
Is Saturday good for you?
How about this Saturday?
I'm afraid I'm busy on Saturday.
I'm afraid I can't make it on Saturday.
Which month is Lena's birthday in?
Which months are the hottest?
When is the rainy season?
When is the dry season?
They sometimes get snow during the winter.
She spends winters in Florida.

Useful words
good   suitable or convenient
make   to be present somewhere

Listen to the conversation: Track 27

Colleagues Brett and Emma are trying to arrange a time to meet.

A It would be good to get together and talk about this.

B Good idea. Are you free any time this week?

A Possibly. Let me look at my planner. What about Wednesday morning?

B No, that's no good. I'm in meetings on Wednesday morning. I could meet you on Wednesday afternoon — before 3 o'clock. Is that good for you?

A Well, I'm meeting a client for lunch in town on Wednesday. We should be finished by 2 :00. But it'll take me half an hour to get back from town, so that wouldn't leave us much time.

B Then let's try another day. How about next Monday or Tuesday?

A Let me see... Monday morning looks good.

B Great. What time?

A How about 10 o'clock?

B 10:00 sounds good. Should I invite Meg? We met a couple of weeks ago to talk about this issue, and I know she's very interested.

A Actually, I'm seeing her this afternoon — I'll mention it to her then, if you like.

B That's a good idea.

A OK, great. See you next Monday at 10:00.

B See you then.

 Listen to more phrases and practice saying them: Track 28

All the phrases by function …

So, to sum up ...

This unit helps you find quickly all the phrases you have learned. You will find all the phrases that are used for the same function in one place under a heading.

Contents

Agreeing and disagreeing

To agree to do something or give someone something, use **Yes** or **OK**. To make **yes** more definite, add **of course**.

> "Will you come with me?" "**Yes**."
> "Could you help me with my bags?" "**Yes, of course**."
> "Can I have ice cream?" "**Yes**."

> "Can you make dinner tonight?" "**OK**, if you like."
> "Will you drive?" "**OK**."
> "Can I borrow your pen?" "**OK**."

If you think that what someone has said is right, say **I agree ...** or **You're right**.

> **I agree**. I think she's great.
> Yes, **I agree** with you. We need to promote him.

> **You're right**. We waste too much food.
> I think **you're right** about the website.

If you feel strongly that what someone has said is right, say **I totally agree ...** .

> **I totally agree**. I think it's terrible.

To say you will not do something or give someone something, use **No**.

> "Could you give me a lift?" "**No**, sorry, I don't have time."
> "Will you pay for the ice cream?" "**No**, it's your turn."

If you think that what someone has said is wrong, say **I disagree ...** and if you feel strongly that what someone has said is wrong, say **I totally disagree ...** .

> I'm afraid **I disagree**. I think it's a really bad idea.
> **I totally disagree**. I think it's a complete waste of money.

If you do not agree with someone's opinion, you can also use **I don't think so.**

> "Pierre's really nice, isn't he?" "**I don't think so.** He never speaks to me."
> "Traveling by train is really relaxing." "**I don't think so.** I prefer to fly."

Apologizing

To apologize, use I'm **sorry ...** or **Sorry ...** .

> **I'm sorry** you were late because of me.
> **I'm sorry** I missed your party.

> **Sorry,** I have to leave now.
> **Sorry,** I didn't hear what you were saying.

To make your apology stronger, use **I'm really sorry ...** or **I'm so sorry ...** .

> **I'm really sorry** I can't help you.

> **I'm so sorry** I upset you.

If you have to tell someone that there is a problem or that something bad has happened, start your sentence with **I'm afraid ...** .

> **I'm afraid** I can't come tonight.
> **I'm afraid** there's a problem with your order.

If someone says sorry to you, you can make them feel better by saying **Don't worry about it.**

> "I'm sorry — I spilled your drink." "**Don't worry about it**."
> "Sorry we're late." "**Don't worry about it** — I just got here myself."

> "Sorry I forgot your birthday." "**Don't worry about it.**"
> "I'm afraid the handle came off the door." "**Don't worry about it** —
>   it happens all the time."

A more informal way to respond to someone saying "Sorry" is **No problem** or **That's OK.**

> "Sorry I can't make it to your party." "**No problem**, I understand."
> "We ate all the food." "**No problem**. I'm not hungry anyway."

> "Sorry about the noise." "**That's OK** — it didn't bother me."
> "I didn't bring a coat." "**That's OK** — I can lend you one."

Asking for and giving explanations

The simplest way to ask for an explanation is to use **Why ... ?**

>**Why** did you say that?
>**Why** don't you like Bella?
>**Why** can't we leave now?

Could you explain ... ? can also be used to ask someone to explain something, especially in a classroom.

>**Could you explain** how volcanos are formed?
>**Could you explain** why you came to this conclusion?

A slightly more informal way of asking for an explanation is **Why is it that ... ?**

>**Why is it that** your hands can be cold while the rest of you is warm?
>**Why is it that** the glacier doesn't melt?

The simplest way of giving an explanation is to use **Because ...** .

>I was late **because** I missed the bus.
>**Because** heat cannot pass from a colder object to a warmer object.

You can also use **The reason is that ...** .

>**The reason is that** trees absorb the carbon dioxide.
>**The reason is that** the second number is larger than the first.

Asking for information

To ask for information, use the question words **Where ... ?**, **When ... ?**, **Why ... ?**, **Who ... ?**, **Which ... ?**, **What ... ?**, and **How ... ?**

>**Where** is your office?

>**When** did you meet Olga?

>**Why** did you leave Tokyo?

>**Who** was there?

Which café was she in?

What's the name of the hotel?

How do I get his address?

To ask someone that you do not know for information, you can use **Could you tell me ... ?** or **I'd like to know ...** .

Could you tell me where the train station is?
Could you tell me how much a ticket to Providence is?

I'd like to know how much a double room would be.
I'd like to know whether you have any three-bedroom houses for rent.

Use **Tell me ...** to ask someone general questions about their life.

Tell me about your trip, Ian. Was it good?
Tell me about work, Yuko. How's it going?

To ask someone to describe someone or something, use **What's ... like?**

What's your hotel **like?**
What's his new manager **like?** Is she nice?

To ask someone to describe a person's appearance, use **What does ... look like?**

What does Jim **look like?** Does he look like his dad?
I don't know which one is Pilar. **What does** she **look like?**

We often use **Is ... ?** to start questions that require information.

Is he tall?
Is it far from the city center?
Is breakfast included?
Is she like her sister?
Is he a good teacher?

To ask questions about a particular thing, for example in a store, use **Is this ... ?** or **Is it ... ?**

> **Is this** the biggest size?
> **Are these** the only colors you have?

> **Is it** made of real leather?
> **Is it** big enough for four people?

To ask if a place has something, use **Is there ... ?** or **Are there any ... ?**

> **Is there** a hairdryer in the room?
> **Is there** a pool?

> **Are there any** good schools near here?
> **Are there any** more blankets in the room?

You could also use **Does ... have ... ?** to ask the same question.

> **Does** the apartment **have** central heating?
> **Does** the hotel **have** a swimming pool?

To ask how to do something, use **How do you ... ?**

> **How do you** get to the old part of town?
> **How do you** know which bus to take?

To ask about time, use **What time ... ?**

> **What time** does he get home?
> **What time** do we have to leave in the morning?

To ask about prices, use **How much ... ?**

> **How much** is the rent?
> **How much** do you charge for Internet service?

To ask about the time that something took or will take, use **How long ... ?**

> **How long** does the tour last?
> **How long** were you waiting?

How's ... ? is used to ask someone's opinion of the quality of something, or whether they are enjoying it.

> **How's** life in Madrid, Jill? Are you enjoying it?
> **How was** the concert?

If you want someone who knows about something to suggest something that might be good or worth having, use **Can you recommend ... ?**

> **Can you recommend** a nearby hotel?
> **Can you recommend** a good service provider?

Use **Can you give me the number ... ?** to ask for the phone number of someone who can provide a service for you.

> **Can you give me the number** of a local dentist?
> **Can you give me the number** of a car service?

If you want to ask someone for advice about something, use **Could you give me some advice ... ?** This phrase is followed by the prepositions **about** or **on**.

> **Could you give me some advice** on how to organize my report?
> **Could you give me some advice** about English courses?

Asking if something is allowed or permitted

To ask for permission, use **Can I ... ?**

> **Can I** pay by credit card?
> **Can I** sit here?
> **Can we** camp here?

A more formal way of asking if something is allowed or permitted is to use **May I ... ?**

> **May I** borrow this travel guide?
> **May I** take this chair?
> **May I** use your phone, please?

If you want to check that someone will not be unhappy or angry if you do something, use **Do you mind if ... ?**

> **Do you mind if** I park here for a moment?
> **Do you mind if** I leave my suitcase here for five minutes?
> **Do you mind if** I get there a bit later?

An informal way of asking for permission is **Is it OK to ... ?**

> **Is it OK to** try a grape?
> **Is it OK to** take the clock out of its box?
> **Is it OK to** leave our bags here?

Asking for things

To ask for something, use **Can I have ... ?**, **Could I have ... ?**, or **I'd like ...** .
To be very polite, use **please**.

> **Can I have** two tickets for tonight's performance, please?
> **Can I have** an audio guide, please?

> **Could I have** a receipt, please?
> **Could we have** three seats together?

> **I'd like** an apartment near the university.
> **I'd like** a map of the area, please.
> **I'd like** to stay three nights.

If it is important for you to have something, you can use **I need ...** .

> I really **need** her address.
> **We need** a guide who can speak English.

To describe the thing you want, use **I'm looking for ...** or **I want ...** .

> **I'm looking for** the bus station.
> **I'm looking for** a place to rent.

> **I want** a light summer jacket.
> **I want** to rent a house for six months.

If you want to ask if something you want is available, use **Do you have ... ?** or **Have you got ... ?**

> **Do you have** any brochures in English?
> **Do you have** any tickets left for tomorrow's show?
> **Do you have** any train timetables?

> **Have you got** any strawberries?
> **Have you got** an extra textbook?
> **Have you got** a bag that I could have?

To ask if a store sells the thing you want, use **Do you sell ... ?**

> **Do you sell** light bulbs?
> **Do you sell** newspapers?
> **Do you sell** fresh bread?

When you have decided what you want to buy in a shop, use **I'll have ...** or **I'll take ...** .

> **I'll have** the strawberry ice cream.
> **I'll have** a half pound of ham.

> **I'll take** these two postcards.
> **I'll take** the blue ones.

If you are asking someone if they can do something for you, use **Can you ... ?** or **Could you ... ? Could you ... ?** is slightly more polite and formal than **Can you ... ?**

> **Can you** tell me what the hours are?
> Please **can you** show me where we are on this map?

> **Could you** call a taxi for me?
> **Could you** get someone to fix the window?

A polite way of asking someone to do something is by saying **Would you mind ... ?**

> **Would you mind** translating this into English?
> **Would you mind** giving me an estimate?
> **Would you mind** emailing me the details, please?

To ask whether something you want is possible, use **Is it possible to ... ?**

> **Is it possible to** exchange these tickets for tomorrow's performance?
> **Is it possible to** get an earlier appointment?
> **Is it possible to** speak to the manager?

Attracting someone's attention

When you are asking for information you may need to get someone's attention before you can ask them a question. To do this, first say **Excuse me**.

> **Excuse me**, is the modern art museum near here?
> **Excuse me**, do you know what time the gardens open?
> **Excuse me**, where can I buy a ticket?

Complaining

To talk about something that is upsetting you, use **There's ...**, and for something you think is missing, use **There isn't ...** .

> **There's** a leak in the ceiling.
> **There are** mice under the floorboards.

> **There isn't** any hot water.
> **There aren't** any clean towels in the room.

If something is not good enough, use **I'm not happy with ...** or **I'm disappointed with ...** .

> **I'm not happy with** the parking arrangements.
> **I'm not happy with** my room.

> **I'm disappointed with** the standard of the food.
> **I was disappointed with** the service.

To say that you think something is bad, use **I think ...** .

> **I think** the beds are really uncomfortable.
> **I don't think** the rooms are cleaned often enough.

Congratulating someone

To show that you are pleased that something good has happened to someone, use **Congratulations!**

>**Congratulations** on your new job!
>**Congratulations** on the birth of your son!
>You graduated? **Congratulations!**

To show that you think someone has done something very well, use **Nice job!**

>**Nice job**, Mercedes!
>"I got that promotion, by the way." "**Nice job!** That's great!"
>"Look, I straightened up all those papers." "**Nice job!**"

Dangers and emergencies

To ask for help because you are in danger, shout **Help!**

>**Help!** I can't swim!
>**Help!** The building's on fire!

To tell someone that they are in danger, shout **Look out!**

>**Look out!** There's a car coming!
>**Look out!** It's falling!

To tell someone to pay attention so that they do not have an accident, use **Be careful ...** .

>**Be careful** on those steps!
>**Be careful!** It's icy outside.
>**Be careful** with those scissors!

Describing people and things

Start general descriptions of things with **It's ...** and of people with **He's/She's ...** .

>**It's** gold with three diamonds.
>**It's** a ladies' watch.
>**It's** a green suitcase with wheels.

He's five years old.
She's Canadian.
He was very tall.

Use **It's made of ...** to say what material or substance something is.

It's made of leather.
It's a small bag, and **it's made of** velvet.
The beads are bright blue, and **they're made of** glass.

Use **He/She has ...** to talk about what someone looks like.

She has short blond hair.
He has a beard.
She has a small mouth.

To talk about someone's clothes, use **He's/She's wearing ...** .

She's wearing jeans and a green T-shirt.
She's wearing an orange blouse.
He's wearing a black jacket.

Encouraging someone

To encourage someone to go somewhere more quickly or to do something more quickly, use **Hurry up!**

Hurry up! We've got to be there in ten minutes!
Hurry up! We're late already!

To encourage someone to go somewhere or to do something more quickly, you can also use **Come on!**

Come on, Helena, or we'll be late!
Come on! We're going to miss our train!
Come on! We haven't got all day!
Come on! Get into the pool. The water's great!

To encourage someone to do something, you can use **Go for it! Go for it!** is informal.

> "I'm thinking of applying for that job." "**Go for it!**"
> "I've decided I want to run a marathon." "**Go for it!**"
> "I'd like to go and see Paolo in New York." "**Go for it!**"

Explaining a problem

To explain a general problem, use **I have a problem ...** . Use the preposition **with** to talk about a thing that is causing your problem.

> **I have a problem** — this work has to be done by tomorrow, but I don't have the books I need.
> **I have a problem with** my essay — it's far too long, and I don't know what to cut.
> **We have a problem with** our central heating.

If you are asking somebody for help, you will need to be able to describe the problem. Use **There's ...** to say what the problem is.

> **There's** water all over the floor..
> **There's** a noise coming from the engine.
> **There are** mice in the kitchen.

If the problem is that you do not have something you need, use **There isn't ...** or **I don't have ...** .

> **There isn't** any soap in the bathroom.
> **There isn't** enough food for everyone.
> **There aren't** any towels in my room.

> **I don't have** her address.
> **She doesn't have** enough money.
> **He doesn't have** a car.

For some problems, you can use **I have ...** .

> **I have** a problem.
> **I have** a flat tire.
> **I have** too much work.

If the problem is that you are not able to do something, use **I can't ...** .

> **I can't** drive.
> **We can't** open the bedroom door.
> **I can't** find my keys.

If you want to say that you do not understand something, use **I don't understand ...** .

> **I don't understand** what he's saying.
> **I don't understand** the instructions.
> **I don't understand** how to use this phone.

If you do not have the knowledge to do something, use **I don't know how to ...** .

> **I don't know how to** get my email.
> **We don't know how to** get there.
> **I don't know how to** change a fuse.

If a piece of equipment will not do what you want it to do, use **The ... won't ...** .

> **The** engine **won't** start.
> **The** barbecue **won't** light.
> **The** shower **won't** work.

Expressing opinions

If you want to give your opinion about something, use **I think ...** .

> **I think** their website is excellent.
> **I thought** he was very reasonable.
> **I don't think** they did a very good job.

You can also give your opinion of something by saying **in my opinion ...** .

> **In my opinion**, these sales targets are too high.
> **In my opinion**, she's in the wrong job.

To ask someone for their opinion, say **What do you think of ... ?**

> **What do you think of** her abilities?
> **What did you think of** the meal?

You can also ask someone for their opinion by saying **What's your opinion of ... ?**

> **What's your opinion of** the company?
> **What's your opinion of** their performance?

To ask someone if they think something is a good idea, use **What do you think about ... ?**

> **What do you think about** going out for dinner tonight?
> **What do you think about** inviting Eva?
> **What do you think about** going to France this year for vacation?

Expressing surprise

A simple way to show that you are surprised by what someone has said is to use **Really?**

> "Zack is leaving?" "**Really?** Why?"
> "I don't think it's a very good school." "**Really?** I was very impressed by it."
> "I'm terrible at math." "**Really?** I can't believe that."

A stronger way to show that you are surprised by what someone has said is to say **That's incredible!** or **That's amazing!**

> You ran twenty miles in two and a half hours? **That's incredible!**
> So Steve works a sixty-hour week? **That's incredible!**

> Camille spent 2,000 dollars on a jacket? **That's amazing!**
> You cooked for sixty people? **That's amazing!**

An informal way to show surprise at what someone has said is to say **You're kidding!**

> "Daniel is leaving." "**You're kidding!** He's only been here for three months!"
> "They're buying a house in Colorado." "**You're kidding!** Another house?"

Expressing sympathy

The most common way to show that you are sad for someone when something bad has happened is to use **I'm (so) sorry** or **I'm sorry to hear ...** .

> Diana told me about your brother's accident. **I'm so sorry.**

I heard that Charlie lost his job, Sara. **I'm sorry.**

I'm so sorry to hear that your mother died.
I was very sorry to hear about Julia and Marco.

To show that you are sorry when something slightly bad or disappointing has happened, use **It's a shame ...** or **It's a pity ...** .

It's a shame you couldn't come with us last night.
It's a shame she didn't graduate after all that hard work.

It's a pity you can't stay longer.
It's a pity your mother won't be there.

Hellos and goodbyes

Use **Hello** as a general greeting. It is polite to say **Hello** to anyone in any situation.

Hello, Jorge.
Hello, Dr. Ahmed.

Use **Hi** in informal situations, for example when you are meeting friends.

Hi, how are things with you?
Hi, how are you doing?
Oh **hi,** Adam. I didn't know you were coming.

Use **Good morning, Good afternoon,** or **Good evening** in slightly more formal situations, for instance if you meet a neighbor or when you see people at work.

Good morning, everyone. Today we are going to learn how to form questions.
Good afternoon, Mr. Kowalski.

Use **Goodbye** when you leave someone.

Goodbye, Clara. Have a safe journey.

Goodbye is often shortened to **Bye ...** .

Bye, everyone!

Use **Goodnight ...** when you are going to bed, or if someone else is going to bed.

> **Goodnight,** everyone — see you in the morning.

See you ... is an informal way of saying goodbye to someone you know you will see again.

> OK, I need to go now. **See you!**
> **See you** tomorrow!
> **See you** on Monday!

If someone has come to a place for the first time, you can use **Welcome!**

> **Welcome!** I'm so pleased you could come.
> **Welcome** to Blakey Publishing!
> **Welcome** to Cambridge!

Introducing people

If you want to introduce someone to someone else, use **This is ...** .

> **This is** my husband, Richard.
> **This is** Medina, my friend from school.
> **These are** my children, Theo, Ruby, and Phoebe.

In slightly formal situations, use **I'd like you to meet ...** or **Can I introduce you to ... ?**

> **I'd like you to meet** Dr. Garcia. Dr. Garcia has been working on our project.
> **I'd like you to meet** our head of department, Elizabeth Miller.

> **Can I introduce you to** my husband, Andre?
> **Can I introduce you to** Omar? He's going to be giving a talk later.

> **GOOD TO KNOW!**
> When you are introduced to someone, you can just say **Hello**, or in a slightly more formal situation, say **Pleased to meet you** or **Nice to meet you.**

Making arrangements

When you make arrangements with someone, you may want to check if they are happy with them. Use **What if ... ?**

> **What if** we meet a little earlier?
> **What if** I met you at the restaurant?
> **What if** we went by train?

To ask someone if they would prefer a different arrangement, use **Would you prefer it if ... ?** or **Would it be better ... ?**

> **Would you prefer it if** we didn't invite Claudia?
> **Would you prefer it if** we came to see you later?

> **Would it be better** to ride our bikes there?
> **Would it be better** if we ate out somewhere?
> **Would it be better** if we took some food with us?

To make sure someone is happy with a plan, use **Is ... OK?**

> **Is** seven o'clock for dinner **OK** with you?
> I was thinking of the Greek restaurant on South Main Street. **Is** that **OK** with you?
> **Is** it **OK** if I don't come?
> **Is** it **OK** to meet after the movie?

Another way to make sure that someone is happy with a plan is to use **How does ... sound?**

> I was thinking we'd meet for dinner and then see a film. **How does** that **sound**?
> What about a week in California ? **How does** that **sound**?
> What about coffee at The Book Shop café, followed by shopping? **How does** that **sound**?
> **How does** eight-thirty for dinner **sound**?

Another way to agree on the time or date of arrangement is to use **Why don't we say ... ?**

> So what time are we meeting? **Why don't we say** eight o'clock — or is that too late?

Lunch at Café Otto sounds cool. **Why don't we say** one o'clock inside the café?

Why don't we say twelve-thirty in the bookstore? Is that OK?

Why don't we say seven o'clock for dinner? Does that work for you?

Making suggestions

One easy way of making a suggestion is to use **We could ...** .

We could go and see a movie.

We could call Rav and see what he says.

We could go for a walk, if you like.

> **GOOD TO KNOW!**
> When people start a sentence with **We could** they often add **if you like**.

If you are eager to do something with someone, use **Let's ...** .

Let's have a party!

Let's buy tickets for Saturday's game.

I've got a good idea. **Let's** all go swimming.

Another way to make a suggestion is to use **Why don't we ... ?**

Why don't we go out for dinner?

Why don't we have a barbecue and invite some friends?

Why don't we get her a present?

If you have an idea, use **How about ... ?** or **What about ... ?**

How about going somewhere for coffee?

How about going bowling?

What about asking Tahir to join us?

What about taking a picnic to the park?

> **GOOD TO KNOW!**
> **How about/What about + -ing**
> A verb that comes after **How about** or **What about** must be in the -ing form.

To suggest what someone else can do or where someone else can go, use **You could ...** .

> **You could** rent an apartment for a while.
> After your meal, **you could** have ice cream on the deck.

You can also use **Why not ... ?** or **Why don't ... ?** if you have an idea about what someone else might do.

> **Why not** ask Melissa to help out?
> If you don't have anything to do, **why not** go to Helena's party?

> **Why don't** we buy a tent?
> **Why don't** you come to the party after the movie?

I suggest ... and **You should ...** are slightly strong ways of making a suggestion.

> **I suggest** we take a taxi there.

> **You should** look online, and see if you can get something cheaper.

Making sure you've understood

If you do not understand what someone has said, use **I don't understand.**

> Sorry, **I don't understand**.
> **I didn't understand** what you said.
> Please could you repeat that? **I didn't understand**.

You can ask for help with understanding by using **Would you mind ... ?**

> **Would you mind** speaking more slowly?
> **Would you mind** repeating that?
> **Would you mind** speaking in English?

To check the meaning of a word, use **What does ... mean?**

> **What does** "fragile" **mean**?
> **What does** "end up" **mean**?
> **What does** "out of order" **mean**?

> **GOOD TO KNOW!**
> If you do not hear what someone has said and you want them to repeat it, use **Pardon?** or **Sorry?**

Please and thank you

When asking for something from someone, use **please**.

> Two oranges, **please**.
> A large apple pie, **please**.
> Could you give these to Jerry, **please**?
> Could I borrow this chair?
> Could you **please** clean up now?

To say that you would like something that someone has offered you, use **Yes, please.**

> "Would you like some more coffee?" "**Yes, please.**"
> "Do you need a bag?" "**Yes, please.**"
> "Can I help you with those bags?" "**Yes, please.**"
> "Would you like me to mail this for you?" "**Yes, please.**"

To thank someone, use **Thank you** or **Thanks**. **Thanks** is slightly informal.

> **Thank you** for all your help, Zalika.
> **Thank you** very much for coming here tonight.
> "Here's a little birthday present." "**Thank you!**"
> "You look great in that dress." "**Thank you**, Judy."

> **GOOD TO KNOW!**
> To make **Thank you** or **Thanks** stronger, use **very much** after it.

> "Here, have a cup of coffee." "**Thanks**, Randy."
> "I love your new haircut." "**Thanks**, Juliana."
> Hey, **thanks** for helping out this weekend, Anneli. I really appreciate it.
> **Thanks** very much for all those books you gave the children. It was very kind of you.

> **GOOD TO KNOW!**
> People often say something extra after saying **thank you** or **thanks** to make it stronger. For example they often say **I appreciate it** or **It was very kind of you** or **It was very nice of you**.

To accept someone's thanks, use **You're welcome** or **Not at all.**

> "Thank you for all your help, John. We appreciate it."
> "**You're welcome.**"
> "Thanks for dinner last night. It was really delicious." "**You're welcome.**
> Any time."

> "Thanks for looking after the children on Saturday – that was a great
> help, Lucia." "**Not at all.**"
> 'Thank you for lending me the book. I loved it." "**Not at all.**"

Another way of accepting someone's thanks is to use **It's my pleasure** or
My pleasure. This is a more formal way of accepting thanks.

> "Thank you for the lovely gifts." "**It was my pleasure.**"
> "Thank you very much for the check, Lucy. It was very kind of you."
> "**It's my pleasure.**"

> "Thank you, Simone." "**My pleasure.**"
> "Thank you, Ben — you've been a great help." "**My pleasure.**"

Another way of accepting thanks from a person that you know is to use
No problem.

> "Thanks for looking after Rosie — it was a great help." "**No problem.**"
> "Thanks for the invitation." "**No problem.**"

Saying what you have to do

To tell someone that it is very important that you do something, use **I have
to ...** or **I need to ...** .

> **I have to** call my mother.
> I really **have to** finish this today.
> **You** don't **have to** work till eight o'clock every evening.

I need to withdraw some money.
I need to cancel that order.
We need to book our flights.

To ask what someone has to do, use **Do you have to ... ?**

Do you have to pay for the work yourself?
Do you have to tell them?

If something is important, you could use **It is important for me to ...** .

It is important for me to pass this exam.
It is important for me to work as hard as possible.

Use **I should ...** to say what is the right thing to do, even if you are not going to do it.

I should call Sergei and let him know.
I really **should** go to the gym.
We really **should** invite both sets of parents.

> **GOOD TO KNOW!**
> There is no "to" after **I should**.

Saying what you like, dislike, prefer

The simplest way to say that you like something is to use **I like ...** . To say that you like doing an activity, use **I enjoy ...** . To ask someone if they like or enjoy something, use **Do you like ... ?** or **Do you enjoy ... ?**

I like painting.
Do you like driving?

I enjoy just looking out of the window.
Do you enjoy exploring new places?

If you like something, but not in a strong way, use **I sort of like ...** .

I sort of like going to the movies.
I sort of like the ballet.
I sort of like exploring new places.

If you want to say that you like something very much, use **I really like ...** or
I love ... .

I really like Italian food.
I really like traveling because you get to see a different way of life.
I really like looking around cities.

I love looking at the scenery from the train.
I love eating out.
I love meeting new people.

To say that you do not like something, use **I don't like ...** , or to say that you
really do not like something, use **I hate ...** .

I don't like flying.
He doesn't like shopping.
They don't like fish.

I hate getting stuck in traffic.
I hate long-distance flights.
I hate winter.

If you want to say that you like one thing more than another thing, use
I prefer ... . To talk about the thing that you like less, use **to** before it.

I prefer going by the train **to** driving.
I do travel on my own but **I prefer** traveling with other people.

Saying what you want to do

To talk about what you would like to do, use **I'd like to ...** or **I want to ...** .

> **I'd like to** get home early tonight.
> **I'd like to** meet your family.

> **I want to** leave by 5:00 this afternoon.
> **I want to** speak to her as soon as possible.

If you are very eager to do something, use **I'd really like to ...** or **I'd love to ...** .

> **I'd really like to** see the Great Wall of China.
> **I'd really like to** take the children to the beach.

> **I'd love to** go to the movies.
> **I'd love to** go hiking in the mountains.

A slightly informal way of saying what you would like to do or have is or **I wouldn't mind ...** .

> **I wouldn't mind** see a movie.
> **I wouldn't mind** getting something to eat.

Use **I'd prefer to ...** or **I'd rather ...** when you want to do one thing more than another.

> **I'd prefer to** go to a local hospital.
> **I'd prefer to** see a female doctor.

> **I'd rather** have the operation next week.
> **I'd rather** spend a little more and get a better place.

Use **Would you prefer to ... ?** or **Would you rather ... ?** to ask someone if they would like to do one thing more than another.

> **Would you prefer to** stay home tonight?
> **Would you prefer to** spend a little less?

> **Would you rather** eat earlier?
> **Would you rather** spend more time with the children?

Talking about your health

After saying hello to someone, especially someone we know, we usually ask about their health, by saying **How are you?**

> Hello, Jan. **How are you?**
> It's great to see you, Anna. **How are you?**

> **GOOD TO KNOW!**
> To answer that question, use **I'm fine, thanks** or **I'm good thanks.**
> If you are not well, you could say **Not great, really** or **Not too good, actually.**

If you need to describe a medical problem, you can use **I have ...** .

> **I have** a temperature.
> **I have** a cold.
> **I have** asthma.

If you want to say which part of your body hurts, use **my ... hurts**.

> **My** back **hurts**.
> **His** foot **hurts**.
> **My** neck **hurts**.

If the pain you have is an ache, you can say which part of your body it is in by using **I have ... ache**.

> **I have** a head**ache**.
> **I have** a stomach**ache**.
> **She has** a tooth**ache**.

You can talk about more general problems that you are having using **I feel ...** .

> **I feel** tired all the time.
> **I feel** sick.
> **I feel** like I'm getting sick.

Talking about your plans

Use **I'm + -ing verb ...** or **I'm going to ...** to talk about plans that you are sure of.

> **I'm spending** a couple of days with my parents.
> **They're going** on vacation this summer, as usual.
> **I'm stopping over** in Thailand on the way there.

> **I'm going to** study in London.
> **I'm going to** travel first-class.
> **I'm going to** take the kids to the park.

Use **Are you going to ... ?** or **Will you ... ?** to ask someone about their plans.

> **Are you going to** go with Tahir?
> **Are you going to** tell Alex?
> **Are you going to** see Sophia while you're in Florida?

> **Will you** manage to do any sightseeing between meetings?
> **Will you** charge us extra for the bigger room?
> **Will you** call me when you get home?

To talk about your plans, you can also use **I'm planning to ...** or, if you are slightly less sure, **I'm hoping to ...** .

> **I'm planning to** spend a few days in Berlin.
> **We're planning to** drive along the coast.
> **Jack and Millie are planning to** visit this year.

> **I'm hoping to** stay in hostels most of the time.
> **She's hoping to** take a tour of the nearby islands.
> **We're hoping to** fit in some skiing while we're in the mountains.

To talk about a plan that is only possible, use **I might ...** .

> **I might** book a room for that night.
> **I might** spend an extra week in Calgary.
> **I might** stay on if I like it there.

To talk about something that should happen in the future, use **I'm supposed to ...** .

> **I'm supposed to** be at the station by 8:00.
> **I'm supposed to** meet Brett in Paris.
> What time **are we supposed to** get there?
> **He's supposed to** drive me to the airport.

Talking about yourself

To say what your name is, use **I'm ...** or, in a slightly more formal situation, **My name's ...** .

> Hi, **I'm** Tariq. I'm a friend of Susie's.
> **I'm** Paul. I'm your teacher for this week.
>
> **My name's** Johann.
> **My name's** Yuko. I'm Kazuo's sister.

To give general information about yourself, use **I'm ...** .

> **I'm** a friend of Paolo's.
> **I'm** married with two children.
> **I'm** training for the Boston Marathon.

You can also give general information about yourself using **I have ...** .

> **I have** some friends who live in Nairobi.
> **I have** relatives in Australia.
> **We have** a cabin by the lake.

To talk about your work, use **I'm ...** with the name of a job, or **I work ...** to say something more general about what you do.

> **I'm** a doctor.
> **I'm** a bus driver.

I **work** for an oil company.
I **work** as a translator.

> **GOOD TO KNOW!**
> If you want to ask someone what their job is, use **What do you do?**

To talk about where you live, use **I live ...** or **I'm from ...** . **I'm from ...** is also used to talk about where you were born and lived as a child, even if you do not live there now.

I **live** in Wales.
We live near Moscow.

I'm from Chicago originally, but I live in Phoenix now.
We're from Atlanta.
My family's from India — my parents moved here in 1970.

> **GOOD TO KNOW!**
> To ask someone where they live, use **Where do you live?** or **Where are you from?**

A more formal way of saying where you live is to use **my address is ...** .

My address is 29 Knoll Road, Austin, TX 78759.
My address in England **is** 6 Green Street, Wellington.
My permanent **address is** 257 West 84 Street, New York, NY 10024.

If you are in a place for a short time, either on vacation or for work, you can say where you are living by using **I'm staying ...** .

I'm staying at the Hotel Tulip.
I'm staying with friends in Budapest.
I'm staying in Paris for a week.

Grammar

Verb tenses

The simple present

The simple present tense is used for things that happen regularly or things that are always true.

> They often **go** to the movies on Saturdays.
> He **watches** a lot of TV.
> I don't **like** coffee.
> The sun **rises** in the east.

It is also used to show the speaker's opinions or beliefs.

> I **think** he's a very good teacher.
> I **don't agree** with that at all.

We also use the simple present for planned future actions with a time adverb, for example to talk about travel plans.

> The train **leaves** at 10:40 a.m.
> Our plan **lands** at 6:30.

The present continuous

We use the present continuous to talk about things that are happening now, at the time when we are talking.

> I can't go with you — I'm **finishing** a report for work.
> He's **cooking** dinner.

The present continuous is also used for talking about temporary situations.

> She's **staying** with friends at the moment.
> He's **working** with Frieda this week.

We also use the present continuous to talk about arrangements for future events.

> I'm **flying** to New York next week.
> I'm **seeing** Milos tonight.

The simple past

The simple past tense is used for single actions in the past.

> I **met** Lucy in the café.
> We **walked** around the park.

It is also used for repeated actions in the past, often with *always*, *never*, or *often*.

> I often **had** lunch with her.
> We always **sent** each other birthday cards.

The present perfect

The present perfect is used to talk about things that happened and continue in the past, or at an indefinite time in the past.

> **I've known** Julie all my life.
> They **have already bought** their tickets.
> **Have** you **bought** your tickets yet?

The present perfect is often used to answer the question *How long … ?* together with *for* to talk about a period of time, or *since* to talk about the length of time from a particular point.

> How long **have** you **lived** in Edinburgh?
> I **have lived** there for fifteen years.
> We**'ve had** this car since 2009.
> We **haven't spoken** to each other since then.

The past continuous

The past continuous is used to talk about things that were in progress at a certain time in the past. It's used with "while" and the simple past or when two activities were happening at the same time in the past.

> What **were** you **doing** at eight o'clock last night?
> I **was waiting** for a bus, and she was standing next to me.
> We **were sitting** in the kitchen when my brother came in.

It is also used to describe a scene in the past, especially in a story.

> It was a dreadful morning — the snow **was** still **falling,** and the wind **was howling** round the house.
> The trees **were beginning** to lose their leaves.

The past perfect

The past perfect is used to talk about things that happened in the past before something else happened or before a particular time.

> **Had** you **seen** her before then?
> No, I **hadn't seen** her.
> She **had** just **made** some coffee when I arrived.

It is often used with a time expression such as *always* or *for several days*.

> We **had** always **wanted** to visit Canada, so last year we decided to go.
> It **had rained** continuously for several days.

The future with "will"

The future with "will" is used to talk about things in the future.

> **I'll come** and see you tomorrow.
> She**'ll** call you later.
> They**'ll** eat at the restaurant.

Modals

Modals are verbs such as **might** and **could**. They express ideas such as possibility, permission, or necessity.

These are the modal verbs, with their negative forms and short forms.

Modal verb	Negative	Negative short form
can	cannot	can't
could	could not	couldn't
may	may not	—
might	might not	
must	must not	

will	will not	won't
should	should not	shouldn't
would	would not	wouldn't

> **Can** you see the lions?
> I **couldn't** find my keys.
> I **may** see Joe tomorrow.
> They said they **might** be late.
> **Should** we take a taxi?
> **Will** Lorna be there?
> You **shouldn't** work so hard.
> **Would** you like an apple?

We also use **need** and **have to** as modals.

> I **don't need to** get any more food.
> He **has to** go to the office.

How modals behave

The form of modals does not change. So, for instance, if you use a modal verb with he/she/it, it does *not* add an "s."

> **She may** be home late.
> **It should** work better now.

Modals cannot be used as a main verb on their own — they must always be followed by another verb. There is no "to" infinitive form for modal verbs. If there is no auxiliary verb (**be** or **have**) before the main verb, the main verb must be in the base form.

> Yes, you **can download** those files tonight.
> You **should try** that new restaurant in town.
> I **may** quit.

If one of the auxiliary verbs **have** or **be** follows the modal verb, the main verb will be in the appropriate present or past participle form.

> I **may have upset** him.
> You **could have looked** for it yourself.
> Janice **might be coming** too.
> Sue **should be** happy about this.

Making negatives with modals

To make a negative, put the word **not** after the modal and before the following verb. Remember not to use "to" before the verb.

> You **shouldn't forget** to call her.
> They **won't leave** their house.

Modal negatives often use short forms, especially in speech and informal writing.

> He **won't give** me the money he owes me.
> We **couldn't** see the screen.

Making past tenses with modals

The past modal forms are shown by the form of the verb that comes after the modal.

> They **might not have seen** the letter.
> I **would have asked** her if I'd known.
> They **should have arrived** earlier.

One of the meanings of **could** is as a past tense of **can**, and one of the meanings of **would** is as a past tense of **will**.

> I **could see** them coming.
> They **couldn't find** the book.
> He **wouldn't tell** us what happened.
> The car **wouldn't start**.

The uses of modals

Modals are used to add particular kinds of meaning.

To express doubt or possibility.

> I **may not be able** to do it.
> I think I **might have caught** your cold.

To express degrees of future possibility.

> I **may be** late home tomorrow evening.
> You **will see** her on Friday at Jackie's house.

To ask for or give permission.

> **May I come in**?
> You **can borrow** my car if you like.

To say that someone is not allowed to do something. This meaning uses **not** or a short form **–n't** after the modal verb.

> You **shouldn't use** this computer without permission.

To say what you think might happen or be true.

> The weather's so bad the flight **could be** late.
> It **might be** all over by the time we get there.

To ask people to do something.

Would you please **close** the door?
Could you **get** me a pen?

Short forms

We often use short forms of words, for example **I'm** (I am), **he'll** (he will), **didn't** (did not). In conversation we almost always use these forms — it would sound strange to say the words in their full form. These forms can also be used in informal writing.

We use an apostrophe (') to represent the missing letters.

These are the short forms we use.
'm = am
's = is or has
're = are
've = have
'll = will
'd = would or had

I'm very happy.
They're having a party.
We've finished our work.
He'll call you later.

's can mean either **is** or **has**.

Brad's busy at the moment. (= Brad is)
He's in the garden. (= he is)
She's seen it before. (= she has)
Who's eaten the cake? (= who has)

'd can mean either **would** or **had**.

> **I'd** like a cup of tea. (= I would)
> He said **he'd** do it later. (= he would)
> **She'd** gone shopping. (= she had)
> **They'd** lost the key. (= they had)

Another common contracted form is **Let's**, which means **let us**. We never use the full form.

> **Let's** to to the beach.
> **Let's** see what Martina says.

Short forms in negatives

Short forms are also used for negatives made with the auxiliary verbs **be, have** and **do**, and with modal verbs such as **can, will** and **must**.

These are the negative short forms made with auxiliary verbs.

be	have	do
isn't = is not	**haven't** = have not	**don't** = do not
aren't = are not	**hasn't** = has not	**doesn't** = does not
wasn't = was not	**hadn't** = had not	**didn't** = did not
weren't = were not		

> My house **isn't** far from here.
> We **weren't** doing anything wrong.
> I **haven't** been to the U.S.
> She **hasn't** seen the movie.
> I **don't** know anything about it.
> They **didn't** like the food.

These are negative short forms made with modal verbs.

can't = cannot	**wouldn't** = would not
couldn't = could not	**shouldn't** = should not
won't = will not	

You **can't** go inside the building.
We **couldn't** find him.
It **won't** rain today.
She **wouldn't** help us.
I **shouldn't** eat so much.

Count and noncount nouns

Count nouns are that we can count. They have singular and plural forms. They can have **a** or **an** in front of them. If they are singular, they *must* have a word like **a**, **an**, **the,** or **his,** in front of them.

She ate **an apple**.
Where should I put **my coat**?

Noncount nouns are things that cannot be counted. They cannot have **a** or **an** in front of them, and they do not have a plural form.

I asked for her **advice**.
Mix **the water** with **the flour**.

Here are some common noncount nouns. Remember that the verb that goes with them must be singular.

advice	furniture	progress
air	happiness	safety
anger	homework	knowledge
beauty	information	money
behavior	luggage	water
damage	meat	work

The **meat was** not cooked properly.
The **damage has** not been repaired.
The **information** he gave us **was** correct.
Her **behavior upsets** everyone.

Some/any

You can use **some** and **any** with plural count nouns and with noncount nouns.

> I'd like **some potatoes**.
> I don't have **any shoes**.
> We need to buy **some furniture**.
> Do you have **any milk**?

Many/a few

You can use **many** and **a few** with plural count nouns, but not with noncount nouns.

> There aren't **many stores** in the village.
> We waited for **a few minutes**.

Much

You can use **much** with noncount nouns but not with count nouns.

> You've given me too **much rice**.
> I **don't have much experience** working in an office.

A lot of

You can use **a lot of** with plural count nouns and with noncount nouns.

> I ate **a lot of** cookies.
> She spent **a lot of** money.

Count and noncount

Some nouns can be used in both count and noncount ways. Compare the following sentences.

Count use	Noncount use
He gave me a box of **chocolates**.	The cake was covered with **chocolate**.
I heard a strange **noise** in the bedroom.	There was too much **noise** to work.
Could you turn on the **light**, please?	Open the curtains to let in some **light**.
He warned them of the **dangers**.	We did not understand the **danger** we were in.

A piece of ...

We use **a piece of ...** with some noncount nouns to form count noun phrases.

> She gave me **a** useful **piece of advice**.
> He brought several **pieces of** his own **furniture** with him.
> This is a wonderful **piece of work**.